WHAT GREAT PRINCIPALS DO DIFFERENTLY

Fifteen Things that Matter Most

Todd Whitaker

EYE ON EDUCATION
6 Depot Way West, Suite 106
Larchmont, N.Y. 10538

Library of Congress Cataloging-in-Publication Data

Whitaker, Todd, 1959–
    What great principals do differently: fifteen things that
       matter most / by Todd Whitaker.
      p.   cm.
    Includes bibliographical references.
    ISBN 1-930556-47-0
     1. School principals.   2. School management and
organization.   3. Educational leadership.   I. Title.

LB2831.9 .W45   2003
371.2'012—dc21   2002075234

Production services provided by:
click! Publishing Services
299 E. Kelso Rd.
Columbus, OH 43202
614.261.4645

DATA ANALYSIS FOR COMPREHENSIVE SCHOOLWIDE IMPROVEMENT
Victoria L. Bernhardt

THE SCHOOL PORTFOLIO TOOLKIT
A Planning, Implementation, and Evaluation Guide for Continuous School Improvement
Victoria L. Bernhardt

NAVIGATING COMPREHENSIVE SCHOOL CHANGE:
A Guide for the Perplexed
Thomas G. Chenoweth and Robert B. Everhart

BOUNCING BACK!
How Your School Can Succeed in the Face of Adversity
Jerry Patterson, Janice Patterson, & Loucrecia Collins

INSTRUCTIONAL SUPERVISION:
Applying Tools and Concepts
Sally J. Zepeda

SCHOOL COMMUNITY RELATIONS
Douglas J. Fiore

HUMAN RESOURCES ADMINISTRATION:
A School-Based Perspective 2/E
Richard E. Smith

THE EMERGING PRINCIPALSHIP
Linda Skrla, David Erlandson, etc.

MONEY AND SCHOOLS 2/E
David C. Thompson and R. Craig Wood

STAFF DEVELOPMENT:
Practices that Promote Leadership in Learning Communities
Sally J. Zepeda

About the Author

Dr. Todd Whitaker is a Professor of Educational Leadership at Indiana State University in Terre Haute, Indiana. Prior to coming to Indiana, he was a middle and high school principal in Missouri. In addition, Dr. Whitaker served as middle school coordinator in Jefferson City, Missouri, where he supervised the development of two new middle schools.

Dr. Whitaker has been published in the areas of principal effectiveness, teacher leadership, change, staff motivation, instructional improvement, and middle-level practices. His books include *Dealing with Difficult Teachers*, *Motivating & Inspiring Teachers*, *Dealing with Difficult Parents (and with Parents in Difficult Situations)*, *Teaching Matters: Motivating and Inspiring Yourself*, and *Feeling Great! The Educator's Guide for Eating Better, Exercising Smarter, and Feeling Your Best*.

He is a highly sought presenter and has made hundreds of state, national, and international presentations. Todd is married to Beth who is a former principal and currently is Associate Professor of Elementary Education at Indiana State. They have served as co-editors of *Contemporary Education*, an international journal. They have three children: Katherine, Madeline, and Harrison.

Table of Contents

INTRODUCTION 1

1 WHY LOOK AT GREAT? 3
   STUDYING EFFECTIVE PRINCIPALS 4

2 IT'S PEOPLE, NOT PROGRAMS 7
   TWO WAYS TO IMPROVE OUR SCHOOLS.......................7
   HOW OPEN CLASSROOMS GOT STARTED 8
   ASSERTIVE DISCIPLINE—THE PROBLEM OR THE
       SOLUTION? 10
   INDIVIDUAL TEACHER DEVELOPMENT 12
   REWARDS—PUNISHMENT OR ENCOURAGEMENT? 12

3 WHO IS THE VARIABLE? 13
   WHO IS THE VARIABLE IN THE CLASSROOM?...............13
   WHAT IF THE STUDENTS DO POORLY?........................14
   HEY, WHO'S RESPONSIBLE FOR THIS SCHOOL?............15
   ARE HIGH EXPECTATIONS IMPORTANT? 17
   HOW DO WE DEAL WITH THE DEMANDS
       OF OTHERS?..18

4 TREAT EVERYONE WITH RESPECT, EVERY DAY,
   ALL THE TIME..21
   WE NEVER FORGET THAT ONE TIME 21
   TWENTY-FOUR STUDENTS ON THE SIDE OF THE
       TEACHER 22
   PERCEPTION BECOMES REALITY—ONE WAY
       OR ANOTHER 23

TAKE A POSITIVE APPROACH EACH DAY 23

TOO MUCH NICE 25

5 THE PRINCIPAL IS THE FILTER 27

HOW IS YOUR DAY GOING?....................................27

THE SENSE OF CALM 28

THE ANGRY PARENT 29

RAISE THOSE TEST SCORES!....................................29

WHEN THE PRINCIPAL SNEEZES 30

STOP THE THUMPING!...30

THE ONE GOAL OF EVERY FACULTY MEETING 31

THIS IS THE WORST GROUP OF KIDS
        WE'VE EVER HAD 31

6 TEACH THE TEACHERS 35

TEACHERS DO THE BEST THEY KNOW HOW 35

THE TEST SCORE DILEMMA 36

THE POOR LECTURER 36

MODELING EFFECTIVE INTERACTION 37

WE CAN'T TEACH FROM THE OFFICE 37

GET TEACHERS INTO EACH OTHER'S
        CLASSROOMS 38

THE TALENT EXCHANGE 40

7 HIRE GREAT TEACHERS...43

THE GREAT PRINCIPAL'S GOAL 43

WANTED: LEADERS!..44

HIRE FOR TALENT..44

EXPERIENCE IS NOT THE BEST TEACHER; THE BEST
        TEACHER IS THE BEST TEACHER..........................46

THERE IS NO PECKING ORDER..................................48

START INDUCTION AT THE INTERVIEW 49

8 STANDARDIZED TESTING 51
    WITHOUT SUCCESS, TESTS BECOME THE SCHOOL........52
    EFFECTIVE PRINCIPALS KEEP TESTING IN
        PERSPECTIVE 55

9 FOCUS ON BEHAVIOR, THEN FOCUS ON BELIEFS................57
    UNDERSTANDING INCENTIVES..58
    LET'S CALL THOSE PARENTS 59
    LET'S PRAISE THOSE STUDENTS 60
    LET'S IMPROVE THOSE INSTRUCTIONAL
        PRACTICES 60

10 LOYAL TO WHOM? 63
    LOYALTY TO THE STUDENTS...63
    WHAT IS BEST FOR THE STUDENT(S)? 63
    WHAT IS BEST FOR THE SCHOOL? 64

11 BASE EVERY DECISION ON YOUR BEST TEACHERS.............67
    WHAT WILL MY BEST TEACHERS THINK? 68
    IMPLEMENTING A NEW IDEA 69
    MY BEST TEACHERS WILL BE "FINE" NO
        MATTER WHAT...70
    HEY, I SAID ONE BOX OF PAPER CLIPS! 71
    THE PRINCIPAL'S PET 72

12 IN EVERY SITUATION, ASK WHO IS MOST
    COMFORTABLE AND WHO IS LEAST COMFORTABLE...........73
    TREAT EVERYONE AS IF THEY WERE GOOD 74
    UNCOMFORTABLE FEELINGS MAKE PEOPLE
        CHANGE—ONE WAY OR ANOTHER.........................77
    PAY FOR PERFORMANCE 78

13 UNDERSTAND HIGH ACHIEVERS 81
    IGNORE MINOR ERRORS 81

AUTONOMY AND RECOGNITION......................................83

TEACHER EVALUATIONS 84

WHAT ABOUT BURNOUT? 85

14 MAKE IT COOL TO CARE...89

MAKE IT COOL TO CARE..89

THE GREAT TEACHER..91

MERRY CHRISTMAS, EVERYONE! 91

WHO ARE THE LEGENDS? 93

TOUCH THE EMOTIONAL SIDE 94

15 DON'T NEED TO REPAIR—ALWAYS DO REPAIR.................97

SOME NEVER NEED TO REPAIR—BUT ALWAYS DO 98

SOME ALWAYS NEED TO REPAIR—BUT NEVER DO 99

I AM SORRY THAT HAPPENED 100

THE HIGHWAY PATROL..101

16 SET EXPECTATIONS AT THE START OF THE YEAR..............105

WE ARE STILL UNDEFEATED 106

WHY EVERY YEAR? 107

TEACHER EXPECTATIONS FOR CLASSROOM
    MANAGEMENT 108

17 CLARIFYING YOUR CORE 113

REFERENCES..117

Introduction

Any principal can fill a bookshelf with books about educational leadership. Any principal can study lists of guidelines, standards, principles, and theories. The best administrators and the worst administrators can ace exams in their graduate classes. The difference between more effective principals and their less effective colleagues is not what they know. It is what they do.

This book is about *what great principals do* that sets them apart. Clarifying what the best leaders do, and then practicing it ourselves, can move us into their ranks.

The book flows from three different perspectives. I have participated in five research studies, each grounded in visits to schools with more effective principals and schools with less effective leaders. This approach allowed us to determine what great principals do that other principals do not. Also, every year I work with more than fifty schools as a consultant. Observing in these schools, visiting with principals, faculty, students, and staff, I have gained insight into the practices that lead to success. The third perspective is very personal: I write about the core beliefs that have guided my own work as a principal.

This book is not meant to prescribe a narrow set of instructions. Instead, it frames the landscape of school from the perspective of great principals. What do they see when they view their schools and the people in them? Where do they focus their attention? How do they spend their time and energy? What guides their decisions? How can we gain the same advantages?

There is no one answer; if there were, surely we'd all have it by now. Education is extremely complex, and so is school leadership. But we can work toward understanding what the best principals do. We can gain insight into how effective we are as leaders. Most of all, we can continue to refine our skills. All of us have this in common with the best principals: No matter how good we are, we still want to be better.

The format of this book is straightforward. An introductory chapter provides context on the importance of learning from the most effective principals. A concluding chapter asks us to center on our own core beliefs. And in between are fifteen chapters—one dedicated to each of the fifteen things that great principals do differently. Each of us can do everything described in this book—everything the best principals do.

1

Why Look at Great?

We often hear that we can learn from anyone. From effective people, we learn what to do; from ineffective people, we learn what *not* to do. Though this advice contains a grain of truth, think about it: How much can we really learn from our ineffective colleagues about being an effective teacher or principal? We already know plenty about what *not* to do. Good teachers already know not to use sarcasm, not to yell at kids, not to argue with teens in front of their friends. Most principals already know that sitting in the office does little to improve instruction in the classroom or student behavior in the hallways. We don't need to visit an ineffective principal's school to learn this. But we can always reap good ideas from successful educators.

Look at it another way: If school leadership were a true/false test, we could raise our scores by looking over the shoulder of an unsuccessful principal and choosing the opposite answer to each question. However, working with people is never as simple as yes-or-no, bad-or-good, true-or-false. Leadership is more like an open-ended essay exam. It won't help much to copy from the least-prepared student; we already know that doodling in the margins or writing "Vicky-4-Ever" won't earn points. On the other hand, although we might not agree with everything in the best student's essay, we could still learn from it. At the very least, we would probably see some new ideas that we could build on. As school leaders, we face a myriad of choices; eliminating the inappropriate options doesn't move us forward.

Here's one more example: Imagine that you have decided to build a rocket and fly to the moon. Now imagine that you have two choices about learning how to do this: You can go to NASA, or you can come by my house on a Sunday afternoon. Well, if you choose the second option, even the most diligent observation is unlikely to advance your lunar mission. Take all the notes you want: Leaning back in the recliner doesn't inspire engine design; none of the buttons on the TV remote leads to liftoff; lemonade in the shade is not rocket fuel. (Does any of this come as a surprise?)

On the other hand, if you decide to visit NASA, how will that help? You might observe that the rockets they build are bigger than your garage. Their budget looks enormous; they have more engineers. Nevertheless, you can probably learn a good deal about the processes and technology that go into a successful launch.

These examples are simplistic, but the lesson is clear. Educators who want to promote good leadership find value in examining what effective principals do that other school leaders do not.

Studying Effective Principals

I have had the good fortune to conduct or participate in five different studies examining effective principals (Whitaker 1993, Whitaker 1997, Fiore 1999, Roeschlein 2002, Turner 2002). In each study, researchers visited two different groups of schools: schools with outstanding principals and schools with less-than-stellar leaders. Though these studies yielded many insights, their greatest contribution to this book was to focus on the question, "What do the most effective principals do that is *different?*" Without visiting less effective sites, we may not have been able to determine the variables that distinguished the effective principals.

For example, if four outstanding principals hang the same banner in the cafeteria—"All students can learn!"—I might conclude that one key to effective leadership is an inspiring banner in the lunchroom. However, if two of the less effective leaders display the same banner, I would reconsider my conclusion. The banner alone does not guarantee success. Of course, this doesn't mean that you should take your own banner down. Nor does it mean that you must mimic every behavior of a very effective principal. Keep in mind, though, that the practices of great principals *do not get in the way of* their success—and you can learn from them.

In addition to the studies described above, my visits at a multitude of schools and my observations of hundreds of principals have affirmed that effective principals do many things that other principals do not. The purpose of this book is to identify some of the specific practices that set apart the outstanding principals. More importantly, the goal is to help all school leaders become more like their most effective colleagues.

I recently participated in a forum that brought together a wide variety of educators to consider the future of the principalship. One of the questions was, "What skills will principals need to be effective in the 21st century?" I was amazed at the responses. The long list of esoteric (and seemingly unattainable) proficiencies included a computer coordinator's understanding of technology, a lawyer's grasp of special education mandates, the wisdom to lift every student to mastery of impossibly high and ever-changing state and national standards, and the best teaching skills in the school. Whew! I had knots in my stomach just listening. No wonder principals feel so much stress.

Then I realized that we were way off course. What we really need is for all principals to be like the best principals. The best principals probably do not have a barrister's background, nor can they assemble a Pentium 4 computer out of an old soda can. But they *do* lead people to accomplish the important work of schools. Like the best teachers, they adapt to change without losing sight of what really matters. Think of it this way: If every teacher in your school were like your best teachers, would you have a great school? Of course you would. And if all schools had leaders like the best principals, the students who walk through their doors each day would face the 21st century with confidence.

2

It's People, Not Programs

Outstanding principals know that if they have great teachers, they have a great school; without great teachers, they do not have a great school. More importantly, all of their audiences take the same view. If my third-grade daughter has a great teacher, I think highly of her school. If her teacher is not great, I see her school as less than stellar—no matter how many awards she wins, no matter how many students earn high test scores, no matter how many plaques adorn the main office. Students share this perspective; if a high-school sophomore has four great teachers each day (out of four!), then believe me, that sophomore will think the school is great. As the quality of teachers drops, so does a student's opinion of the school. All the way from kindergarten through college, the quality of the teachers determines our perceptions of the quality of the school.

Two Ways to Improve Our Schools

School improvement is actually a very simple concept. However, like many other simple concepts, it is not easy to accomplish. There are really two ways to improve a school significantly:

7

1. Get better teachers.
2. Improve the teachers you have.

We can spend a great deal of time and energy looking for programs that will solve our problems. Too often, these programs do not bring the improvement or growth we seek. Instead, we must focus on what really matters. It is never about programs; it is always about people. This does not mean that no program can encourage or support improvement of people within our school; however, no program inherently leads to that improvement. Believe me, if there were such a program, it would already be in place in every one of our schools.

Each of us can think of many innovations that were touted as *the* answer in education. Too often, we expect them to solve all our woes. When they do not, we see them as the problem. However, we must keep in mind that *programs are never the solution, and they are never the problem.* If we cling to the belief that programs are the solution or the problem, we will continually lose sight of what really makes a difference. Back to basics—whole language—direct instruction—assertive discipline—open classrooms—the Baldridge model—state standards—mission statements—goal setting—site-based management: There is nothing inherently right or wrong with any of these ideas. We may have a fondness for one that has met with success, or deep-seated resentment because another has been forced down people's throats. If we take a closer look at some examples, however, we might see what effective principals never forget: It is people, not programs, that determine the quality of a school.

How Open Classrooms Got Started

Some of you may know the true history of the open classroom movement. I do not claim any expertise about this topic—but for what it's worth, I'll share my vision of how the concept took off.

The scene is an elementary school in Anywhere, USA. At the faculty meeting just before the start of school, the principal announces that he has good news and bad news. The good news: Enrollment is higher than anticipated. The bad news: He needs a teacher to volunteer to teach in the old auxiliary gymnasium. Awkward silence; every teacher avoids eye contact with the principal. Finally, someone raises her hand to volunteer—and not surprisingly, it's Mrs. Smith, the school's best teacher.

Some teachers, in her shoes, might block off a classroom-sized rectangle and keep the students inside it. But this dynamic teacher uses every inch of space, even creating homey nooks and crannies. Then (as often happens in rapidly growing schools), within weeks the principal makes another announcement: He needs to move another class into the gym.

After a little hemming and hawing, guess who raises her hand? The second best teacher in the school, Mrs. Jones. Together, these outstanding teachers create a phenomenal environment in that old musty gym—so much excitement, energy, and engagement in learning that it gives you goose bumps just to walk in.

Later that year, visitors to Anywhere Elementary School walk around to all the classrooms. Where do they see the best teaching and learning? That's right! In the old auxiliary gym. They conclude that open classrooms are the secret to good teaching—and the rest is history.

Ironically, the cycle has come around; now everyone looks askance at open classrooms. Granted, some teachers—especially those who lack solid classroom management skills—may struggle in this environment. What's more, the noise they and their students generate may keep anyone else from sharing space with them effectively. And yet for some of the most dynamic and creative teachers, the open classroom may easily be the *best* teaching environment.

What really energized the Anywhere Elementary School gym was the presence of excellent teachers, not the absence of walls dividing their classrooms. As leaders, we must understand that programs are not solutions. We must adopt changes only if they make our teachers better. Here is another all-too-common example involving a classroom management approach.

Assertive Discipline—The Problem or the Solution?

Classroom management is a common topic for debate. Most of us know of schools that mandate or outlaw certain approaches. Writers and conference speakers on the topic of classroom management often take a similarly polarizing view, hailing certain classroom management techniques as the best, the most appropriate, while rejecting others as inherently inappropriate in our schools.

I'd like to describe two scenarios involving one of these approaches: assertive discipline. All of us are probably familiar with some version of assertive discipline. Typically, if a student misbehaves the teacher writes the student's name on the board. If the same student misbehaves again, the teacher puts a checkmark by the name. For each instance of inappropriate behavior, the teacher adds another checkmark. Specific, predetermined consequences apply for various numbers of checkmarks.
Some people swear by this approach; others swear at it. I have worked with many schools and districts that require assertive discipline and many that officially oppose it. I believe that these schools and districts, in viewing assertive discipline as either a solution or a problem, have lost sight of the critical factor: the teacher.

Mrs. Hamilton was the best teacher I ever worked with. I had the good fortune to spend seven years in the same school with her as an assistant principal and then principal. During that time, I made at least two hundred informal visits to her classroom. In a casual conversation just before I moved out of state to take another position, Mrs. Hamilton mentioned that she was thinking of not using assertive discipline in her class the next year. I was stunned; *I had never known* that she used assertive discipline. Why did I not know? Well, I rarely saw anyone's name on the board, and I never noticed a student's name with a checkmark beside it. Her classroom management skills were as polished as her teaching.

Mrs. Hamilton did not see assertive discipline as a necessary classroom management approach. However, if before she came to her own conclusions, I had decided that assertive discipline was wrong and banned it from our school, would that have helped her as a teacher? If assertive discipline gave her confidence, then the students and our school were better for it.

Now, you may be thinking that assertive discipline seems to be the best approach. Of course, if this were true, every teacher would use it and thrive in their classrooms. Well, I'd like you to meet Mr. Lewis, a teacher from my first year as a principal.

In the second week of school, I decided to make the rounds of my teachers' classrooms. At twenty-six—younger than every teacher in the school—I was a little hesitant to visit classes, but I knew that this was the best way to help improve instruction. So, I walked into Mr. Lewis's third-period English class. I quickly realized that he was quite familiar with assertive discipline. On the board were the names of about a dozen students. The last one was Ricky—written in letters a foot high, with at least five checkmarks, each one larger than the one before. The last checkmark was three feet tall from point to tip. At the board, hunched over like a leprechaun, Mr. Lewis was aggressively gesturing toward the student, "Come on! You want another one?"

Clearly, assertive discipline was not working here. I might have tried to find a "better" technique, but this would merely have placed a new, equally ineffective bandage over the same gaping wound. Assertive discipline was not the problem; Mr. Lewis was the problem. On the other hand, while assertive discipline was not a problem in Mrs. Hamilton's classroom, neither was it the solution. Mrs. Hamilton was the solution.

Educators have seen this pattern repeated many times. The whole-language–phonics debate offers another example. When we took basal readers away from every single teacher, we took away the support that some teachers needed just to survive in the classroom. However, by requiring all teachers to center on phonetics, we may have lost some of the best instruction that others had to offer.

All principals are aware that the students in their schools have individual needs. Great principals are even more aware that their faculty members vary in their individual abilities. Effective principals focus on the people in their schools. They see programs as solutions only when the programs bring out the best in their teachers.

Individual Teacher Development

In one of the studies of principals described previously, teachers in the more effective principals' schools reported that their leaders encouraged and supported individual staff development (Whitaker 1997). Regardless of the need for and commitment to whole-school growth, these principals did everything they could to promote the effectiveness of each individual staff member as a way to improve the school. Ineffective principals paid much less attention to allowing or supporting individual growth. Instead, they focused their efforts on whole-school goals and issues. As school leaders, we must recognize that no matter what programs we introduce or seek to strengthen, our most important work is to improve the people in our schools. Nothing makes as much difference as the quality of our teachers.

Rewards—Punishment or Encouragement?

Much attention has been given recently to the debate over praise and rewards for students. Like many issues, its merits cannot be decided by discussion alone. Otherwise, by now we would know whether praising or rewarding students actually motivates them to do better. Some of our best teachers praise and/or reward their students; so do some of our least effective teachers. What matters is not whether they do it, but how appropriately and effectively they do it.

Ineffective teachers and leaders consistently think they can force or bribe others to do what they want. We all know the diminishing returns of this approach. Effective people build relationships; then others are eager to please them. As a leader, you must make every effort to understand what the deciding factors are—or, to be more precise, *who* the deciding factors are. Effective principals focus on people, not programs.

3

Who Is the Variable?

What really makes the difference between two schools? What matters most in the classroom? Effective principals understand the answer to these questions; indeed, they know that the real issue is not *what* is the variable, but *who*. Great principals know who is the variable in the school; they make all teachers aware of who is the variable in the classroom. Let's examine the classroom first.

Who Is the Variable in the Classroom?

How many of you could predict which teacher in your school will send the most students to the office next year? How about the year after that? When I ask a roomful of principals this question, pretty much every hand goes up. I then ask, "How can you possibly know this? Do you already have the student rosters made up?" The answer is very simple: They know because the main variable in a classroom is *not* the students. The main variable is the teacher.

Interestingly, if I ask *teachers* the same questions, they have the same response. (Generally, the only teachers who don't raise their hands are the two or three who send the most students to the office.) Now, if principals know this, and teachers know this, we ought to be able to talk about it. I have always believed that if there is an elephant in the room, it's important to acknowledge its presence—not just tiptoe around it, pretending it isn't there. Understand, that does not mean we attack the portly pachyderm, or make fun of it—just that we recognize it and take steps to deal with it.

Effective principals work to help all staff members understand the impact they have in their own classrooms. Here is another way to clarify the concept of teacher as variable.

What If the Students Do Poorly?

I would encourage you to explore this issue with your faculty. I'll give you a series of questions to ask at a faculty meeting. (Don't worry—I can tell you the answers in advance. Any group of teachers responds the same way.) Here's a typical dialogue:

> If the best teacher in a school gives a quiz, test, or homework assignment and the kids do poorly on it (and, as we are all aware, this can happen to the best of us), whom does she blame?
> *The predictable answer: Herself.*
>
> Now, if the worst teacher in a school gives a quiz, test, or homework assignment and the kids do poorly on it (and, as we just acknowledged, this can happen to the best of us), whom does she blame?
> *Typical answers: The kids, or the parents, or the administration ("If we had some discipline around here maybe we could teach these kids something"), or last year's teachers, or drugs, or MTV, or . . .*
>
> Whose behavior can a teacher actually control in his classroom?
> *The usual answer: His own.*
>
> The answers speak for themselves.

What is the variable here? Not the students doing poorly on the assignment; that happens in both groups. The variable is *how the teachers respond.* Good teachers consistently strive to improve, and they focus on something they can control—their own performance. Other teachers wait for something else to change. Great teachers look to themselves for answers; poor teachers look elsewhere. As we know, they can wait a very long time for anything else to make a difference.

Clearly, the best teachers accept responsibility for their classrooms, and the worst teachers do not. Effective principals constantly work to make all teachers accept responsibility. More than that, they accept a higher level of responsibility themselves.

Hey, Who's Responsible for This School?

Some years ago I conducted a study involving 163 middle schools (Whitaker 1997). I identified four schools with "more effective" principals and four schools with "less effective" principals. (That is, principals were one standard deviation above or below the group norm based on teacher responses to the Audit of Principal Effectiveness, a nationally normed assessment of principal skills and teacher responses measured by NASSP's Comprehensive Assessment of School Environments (CASE) instrument.) Each group of four schools included an urban school, a suburban school, a small-town school, and a rural school.

On-site visits and interviews with teachers and principals revealed three key differences between the more effective and less effective principals. One critical difference was that *effective principals viewed themselves as responsible for all aspects of their school.* Though these principals regularly involved staff, parents, and others in decision making, they believed it was their responsibility to make their school the best it could be. Regardless of whether situations arose within the school or as a result of outside factors such as budget cuts or school board decisions, the more effective principals saw themselves as the ultimate problem solvers.

The less effective principals more often saw factors outside the school as keys to teacher morale, program development, and staff input. They were much more willing to blame outside influences for problems in their schools, and they felt that they had no control over the outcome.

For example, both of the suburban middle schools I studied were facing significant budget cuts for the upcoming school year. The less effective principal, when discussing the cuts, chose to be critical of the board members and central office administration, with statements such as, "There's not much use trying to help kids when others cut your financial support." The teachers in the school echoed these sentiments and seemed to share their leader's lack of interest in making an effort for their students.

The other suburban school had just been informed of a much more significant budget cut. With a population of 650 students, an approximately 30–to–1 student/teacher ratio, and no assistant principal, they were losing their librarian, their counselor, and four certificated staff. This would raise their student/teacher ratio by two to four students per class. However, the principal had already worked out a strategy to keep the library open; in a school service project, eighth-grade students would take turns staffing the library. In addition, the school planned to enhance its advisory program to offer many of the services that the counselor had provided. Though very disappointed at the budget cuts, the principal chose to focus on a student-centered solution. The teachers shared the same perspective in their interviews.

In a parallel study involving more effective and less effective elementary-school principals, M. E. Whitaker (1997) posed the question, "Who is responsible for the climate in your school?" The more effective principals responded, "I am." The less effective leaders responded, "The teachers are," "We all are," or "Everybody is." These studies not only support the findings that the principal is the decisive element in the school; they also reinforce the fact that effective principals *know* that positive change in their schools is up to them.

A hypothetical scenario brings home the importance of the building principal. Let's say that in two years your child will enter first grade. However, you must enroll your child *now* in one of two schools. You have only one piece of information: One school has a weak faculty but just appointed a truly outstanding principal; the other boasts a strong teaching staff but just hired a very poor principal. If you had to decide today, which school would you choose for your own child two years from now? In my experience, more than ninety percent of educators respond that they would send their child to the school with the great principal. They believe that in two years (or in some cases two months!), the school with the better leader will be the better school.

Are High Expectations Important?

Many people believe—and I agree—that great teachers have high expectations for students. However, let's focus on the question, "What is the variable?" True, your best teachers have high expectations for students. But is this a *difference* that separates great teachers from the rest?

Even your *worst* teachers have high expectations for students. They expect students to be engaged no matter how irrelevant the material is. They expect students to pay attention no matter how boring and repetitious their classes are. They expect students to be well behaved no matter how the teacher treats them. Now, *those* are high expectations.

The variable is not what teachers expect of students; many teachers of all skill levels have high expectations for students. The variable—and what really matters—is *what teachers expect of themselves*. Great teachers have high expectations for students but even higher expectations for themselves. Poor teachers have high expectations for students but much lower expectations for themselves. Not only that: They have unrealistically high expectations for everyone else as well. They expect the principal to be perfect, every parent to be flawless, and every one of their peers to hold them in incredibly high regard.

The same key point applies to principals. All principals—including our most effective and our least effective colleagues—have high expectations for their teachers. The difference between average and great principals lies in *what they expect of themselves*.

How Do We Deal with the Demands of Others?

Interestingly, this concept of accepting responsibility is not limited to education, though at times it may seem so. We constantly hear or read criticisms of schools, teachers, and principals. To survive, we must put these in context. Others, including our critics, focus on their own situations and needs. By the same token, everyone's effectiveness depends at least in part on what they expect of themselves, not of others.

A few years ago, the chamber of commerce in my community held a meeting whose purpose was billed as "enhancing dialogue and communication between businesses and education." The superintendent asked me, as a principal, and two teachers in my school to represent the school district. I was flattered—until we walked into the room. Around a large circular table sat approximately 15 business "leaders." The three of us were the only representatives from the education community. To start the conversation, the business leaders shared their perceptions of "the problem with education nowadays." One by one, they vented their frustrations. "We hire these people and they can't add or subtract," whined the first one. His buddy chimed in, "We hire these people and they can't read or write." The litany went on and on: "We hire these people and their attendance is terrible," "We hire these people and they can't get along with authority." What a treat for my teachers and me!

After about 25 minutes, it finally got to me. I spoke from the heart.

"Your concerns seem to be following a pattern. We hire these people and they can't add or subtract, read or write, show up on time, follow instructions . . ."

The business leaders nodded aggressively.

I looked at them and asked, "Who hires these people?"

I went on: "I used to be a high school counselor, and I never received one call from a potential employer requesting a reference for a student. If you need a way to determine whether an applicant can add and subtract, we can provide old-fashioned worksheets to do that in fifteen minutes. But that's not my biggest issue. What is the variable here?"

I was on a roll. They had touched a core belief of mine—accepting responsibility—and I wasn't about to let them get away with holding others to a higher standard than they applied to themselves.

"How come, with four McDonalds in town, two have great service and two have very rude employees? Ask for help in one of the grocery stores—on the east side of town, you'll get a friendly smile, and on the west side you'd think you were offering someone a root canal. What makes the difference? All six of these stores hire from the same pool of candidates. All of them pay the same wages. *What is the variable?*

"We all know the answer: It's the effectiveness of those who are managing the businesses. And, amazingly, those effective managers assume *it is up to them* to hire and train quality employees—just as the effective teachers assume they are responsible for the students in their classes, even though they have no voice in selecting them.

"Now, instead of blaming, let's see how we can work together so that all of us can be more productive and effective in what we do."

Whew! I needed to say that—and to their credit, they listened.

Accepting responsibility is an essential difference between more effective and less effective employers, teachers, principals—even parents. (Which parents take responsibility for setting expectations about their children's behavior? Which are quickest to blame others?) As principals, we must examine our own acceptance of responsibility. More than that: As leaders, we must help all our teachers take responsibility for their performance in the classroom. If everyone looks in the mirror when they ask, "Who is the variable?" we will have made tremendous strides toward school improvement. This empowering approach raises the level of teacher efficacy and will eventually be passed on to students. Success in any profession starts with a focus on self. After all, we are the one variable that we can most easily and most productively influence.

4

Treat Everyone with Respect, Every Day, All the Time

One of the hallmarks of effective principals is how they treat people. Like effective teachers, effective principals treat people with respect. Now, it's not difficult to treat *some* people with respect, or even to treat *most* people with respect. It's even possible to treat *all* people with respect quite a bit of the time. The real challenge is to treat everyone with respect every day—and great principals do.

We Never Forget That One Time

Each of us can remember at least one occasion in our professional lives when someone in a leadership role treated us inappropriately. No matter how long ago it was, or how often that person treated us well, we remember. The same thing is true in our schools. If just once in a month, or even once in a year, we choose to make a sarcastic comment or cutting remark to a student or staff member, we might as well have carved it in stone. They may pretend to have forgotten that moment, but

21

they will never forget. What's more, anyone else who witnessed it will probably remember too.

This is true not only for our faculty, but also for all of the students in our classrooms. Let's look at an example.

Twenty-Four Students on the Side of the Teacher

It is the first day of school, and we are invisible observers in Mr. Johnson's first-period social studies class. Of the twenty-five students in the room, twenty-four seem to be on their best first-day-of-school behavior. But one—we'll call him #25—is not settling in quite as well. As a matter of fact, he is downright uncooperative and rude.

At this point, assuming no other dynamics are yet established, the other twenty-four students are on Mr. Johnson's side. They want him to take steps so #25 will stop misbehaving. However, since #25 is one of them, they have special expectations. They do want #25 to stop misbehaving, but they want Mr. Johnson to deal with him in a professional and respectful way. As long as he does, they will stay on his side. However, the first time he treats #25 in a less than professional manner—regardless of #25's behavior—the other students will side with #25. Maybe not all of them will shift their allegiance right away, but some will, and now Mr. Johnson has several #25s on his hands. If this happens often, eventually the class will consist of twenty-five #25s—and not one student on Mr. Johnson's side.

The same applies to the principal's interactions with students, parents, and staff members. In general, people know the difference between right and wrong, and they want their leaders to deal with irresponsible peers. If you *always* respond appropriately and professionally, everyone else will be on your team. But the first time you do not, you may lose some of your supporters—and you may never get them back. This makes maintaining a high level of dignity, especially under pressure, a critical skill. Effective principals have this skill; others do not.

Perception Becomes Reality—One Way or Another

In my talks to educators, I often give this example from my years as a principal. Every year, it was my practice to remind my faculty: "You don't have to *like* the students; you just have to *act as if* you like them." The reason is simple: If you don't act as if you like them, then it doesn't matter how much you like them. And if you act as if you like them, then whether you like them at all becomes irrelevant.

Think of the best teachers in your school. Do they like some of their students less than others? Of course they do. But ask yourself this: How do they treat the students they like least? Well, the best teachers treat them just like all the other students. Every student might as well be their favorite student. Whether they like a student or not, they *act as if* they do.

Now think of the worst teachers you have known. Surely they had students they liked—some better than others—but from their behavior, you would think they didn't like any students very much at all! Our behaviors are much more obvious than our beliefs. We will expand on this concept a little later in the book, but it is important in the context of how we treat people every day of the year.

Take a Positive Approach Each Day

One of the key responsibilities of an effective leader is to create a positive atmosphere. So many things can bring teachers down: an upset parent, a troubled student, limited resources. These are facts of the job (and of life). As leaders, our role is to continually take a positive approach. In particular, effective leaders understand the power of praise.

In other books, I have outlined some techniques for effective praise (Whitaker et al. 2000). I won't repeat them all here, but I will focus on one central concept: Praise must be *authentic*. This doesn't mean that praise must be reserved for genuine world-record performances. It just has to be true, that's all.

Nobody minds hearing praise. As a matter of fact, if we praise correctly *it is impossible to praise too much*. And if you question this, just think: Have you ever been praised too much? Of course not. You may have been falsely flattered by someone you knew was not genuine, but if the praise is authentic, it's never too much.

When I work with educators, I often remind them that how much we praise is a choice. And what's more, every time I praise someone, at least two people feel better—and one of them is *me*. Then why are principals and teachers so hesitant to praise? Here are some of the most common responses I get from principals and teachers when I ask why they do not praise more. Let's examine this thinking.

Reason: If I praise people, they will stop working.

Response: If students say how much they enjoy your class, do you slack off and show a video the next day? No, you try even harder. Which comment is more likely to keep you on a diet: "You're looking good," or "It's about time"? If a neighbor compliments you on the lawn you just mowed, do you mow it less carefully next time? Quite the opposite. Next time you might even trim! If you question whether praise works, come on over to my house and look at—my neighbor's lawn.

Authentic praise is a powerful reinforcer and motivator.

Reason: If I start praising people, I might miss someone and hurt their feelings.

Response: Is it better never to praise anyone? If we miss everyone, whose feelings do we spare? And maybe it's not *their* feelings we are worried about; perhaps *we* don't want to feel bad because we left someone out, or perhaps we are unsure of their response so we don't take a chance. People who resent praise given to others do so mainly because they don't feel valued themselves. The solution is not less praise, but a much more inclusive and generous effort to recognize others. As we will see in a later chapter, praise is one key to working effectively with high achievers.

Reason: I don't have the time.

Response: After all, we barely have time to get in all the griping, whining, and complaining we need to do, now don't we? (Sorry, was that sarcasm?)

Name the three teachers in your school who praise the most. Now, name the three best teachers in your school. Is there any overlap there?

I don't know about you, but I would love to be treated the way the best teachers treat their students. Getting called *sir* or *ma'am*, always hearing *please* and *thank you*, and consistently being treated with respect and dignity sounds awfully nice to me.

The principal who sets a positive tone can influence the interactions of everyone in the school. We must make sure we do this even when we least feel like it (and remember, praising others helps us to feel like it). Focusing on all of the positive things in our schools—and there are many—gives us more drive and energy to get through the less positive times. If we do not set this positive tone, who will? And if we do not establish a productive focus, should we be surprised if the voices of the naysayers set quite a different tone?

Too Much Nice

I know that everyone reading this book faces a multitude of demands—and the demands are growing. Special education, alternative education, drug-free education, sex education, and of course the new state standards—all affect our schools and our responsibilities. Each of these may even be essential. We could debate forever about whether we have enough of one or too much of another. But I know one thing for sure: We never have too much nice.

Effective principals understand that one of a teacher's most important tasks is to model appropriate behavior. With all the challenges we face in school, and sometimes at home, being nice to others may seem trivial; but if our classrooms and schools can have that as a foundation, many of the other challenges become less daunting. Principals who consistently model their expectations for how people should be treated give their schools a valuable gift—a gift that, in time, everyone in the school can give to each other.

If everyone in a school is treated with respect and dignity, you may still have nothing special. However, if everyone in a school is not treated with respect and dignity, you will never have anything special. Of that, I am sure.

5

The Principal Is the Filter

Effective principals understand that they are the filters for the day-to-day reality of school. Whether we are aware of it or not, our behavior sets the tone. If people see us running down the hallway screaming *Fire!*, it will be the talk of the school for days, even if it was a false alarm. By the same token, if we calmly ask people to escort their students out of the building, the students will evacuate just as quickly, but without spreading panic throughout the school. The most effective principals choose their filters carefully.

How Is Your Day Going?

As principals, we hear this question many times a day. Our response not only influences how others view us, but also affects the frame of mind of the person who asked. What's more, we have choices about how to respond.

You can smile at a teacher and say, "Things are great! How about with you?" Or you can respond, "That Jimmy Wallace is getting on my nerves!"—and all of a sudden Jimmy Wallace is getting on that teacher's nerves too (whether the teacher knows him or not).

You may be thinking that you could not do this because you would never lie. Hmm: So when the second graders ask if you like the mural they drew, what do you tell them? How do you answer the question, "Honey, do these pants make me look fat?" Again, it is always up to us to determine what gets through our filters and what does not.

The Sense of Calm

I was recently the speaker at a state principals' conference. The morning went very well. At the luncheon, the lobbyist for the state association spoke. Gruffly taking the microphone, he said, "I am doing my best to lobby the state legislature this session, but you need to know something. There is potentially some bad legislation out there, bad legislation." Then he sat down. You could have heard a pin drop. The energy in the room drained away. Bad legislation—what does that mean? Are they going to mandate the metric system for all grades? Are the Russians beating us in the space race again? Are they going to take our oldest child? Apparently we would never know.

What had happened? Well, this gentleman was the filter between the state legislators and the principals' association. He had choices about what to share and what to filter out. He chose to filter out the fact that this was just potential legislation, most of which falls by the wayside every year. He chose to filter out any specifics about the workings of the potential new laws. He chose to filter out the fact that some pro-school efforts were also taking place. And he chose to filter out what the group could do about it.

By dropping bad-news grenades on the group, the lobbyist quite unintentionally broke everyone's spirit. Not only did he discourage them about prospects for the future; he also took away their eagerness to go back to their schools the next day. Ironically, no one would accuse him of lying, yet his selective truths were much more damaging than telling the second grade students that you liked their mural. We are all filters for our school, and it is up to us to determine what kind of filter we want to be.

The Angry Parent

Here's another scenario, filtered two ways. Let's examine what happens under each.

Say I'm a principal, meeting with an irate parent in my office behind closed doors. As so often happens, Mrs. Smith is really mad at the world; I just happen to be the one sitting there as she vents her feelings. After she leaves, I walk into the hall and a teacher says innocently, "How is your day going?" Now I have choices to make.

I can choose to filter my response: "Things are great, how about with you?" If that teacher feels good about the world, we both move on, smiling. If the teacher has concerns, at least I have not made them worse.

Or I can respond, "Oh, I just met with that out-of-control parent Mrs. Smith. Man, she has some temper! I hope I never have to deal with her again. Yikes!" Now, what have I accomplished? Well, I have made that teacher terrified of Mrs. Smith. And if I tell enough people about Mrs. Smith, I might have every teacher in the school worrying about the possibility of meeting this notorious harridan. Some might be leery of working with any student whose last name is Smith, or hesitant about calling any parents (and especially the ones named Smith). I have shifted their energy away from confidently approaching their students to unproductive worrying.

One way or the other, my response affects the school. By sparing others the unnecessary bad news, I can create a much more productive environment. This applies not only to working with people outside the school, but also to working with people within our district.

Raise Those Test Scores!

Many—probably too many—of us have been to a meeting at our central office where a district administrator ranted and raved about some situation in need of improvement. A fairly common example might be our school's or district's scores on standardized state tests. (The all-too-familiar chant—"Raise those test scores!"— reminds me of a track coach yelling, "Run faster!" If we want our athletes to run faster, we need to teach them how. The same applies to raising test scores.)

In any case, how we respond to such tirades during that meeting is one thing; more critical is what we do—how we filter events—when we come back to our school. If a teacher asks, "How was the meeting at central office?" I would respond, "Fine. How are you doing?" Of course, we would continue our effort to increase student achievement, but I would avoid a knee-jerk reaction that would only lead to widespread disgruntlement.

When the Principal Sneezes

When the principal sneezes, the whole school catches a cold. This is neither good nor bad; it is just the truth. Our impact is significant; our focus becomes the school's focus. If we have great credibility and good relationships, people work to please us. If we lack credibility, people work against us. Once we make it clear what we want, supporters will work for it and opponents will drag their feet or head the other way. The relations we establish will determine how many are in each camp. We must keep our attention on the issues that matter, not divert our effort and energy to trivial annoyances.

Stop the Thumping!

Visiting a middle school a few years ago, I was sitting in the back of a very effective teacher's classroom. The class was quietly focused on important projects. Suddenly, a whole-school announcement came over the loudspeaker. Interrupting every class in the building, the principal issued the following proclamation:

"Students in this school must immediately stop thumping! There have been too many students in the school thumping other students. Thumping is when you pull back your middle finger with your thumb and then release it so that it strikes another person sharply in the chest. We will have no more thumping in this school. Anyone caught thumping should be sent to the office."

Well, as I looked around the room, not one student was still focused on the project. Instead, 29 students were practicing some form of "thumping" on themselves or on a partner. In fact, I soon realized that I too was sitting there thumping myself, just to see what it felt like. This was a classic example of the principal being the filter—just not in the most positive way.

The One Goal of Every Faculty Meeting

I really like faculty meetings; I always have. As a principal, I cherished the opportunity to spend time with an outstanding group of professionals. Because that time is precious, it's crucial to make the most of it. Like you, I tried not to waste time in staff meetings reading announcements or working on logistical matters that could be handled in writing. Furthermore, like you, I understood that these regular meetings offer an opportunity for staff development. But no matter what the purpose, content, or focus of the faculty meeting might be, I always had one simple additional goal: *I wanted the teachers to be more excited about teaching tomorrow than they were today.*

You can make this a goal for faculty meetings and for other, less formal meetings as well. Consciously or not, *you* decide how to end any meeting. Your decision to end on a positive note will send others to their next challenge with energy and enthusiasm. If you do not work to determine the climate of your school, believe me, somebody else will. Great principals know that putting others in an upbeat frame of mind comes back to brighten their own day as well. Keeping your school in a positive cycle enhances everything you do.

This Is the Worst Group of Kids We've Ever Had

Have you ever heard this refrain? It seems that the same two or three teachers start the chant at about the same time each year. They are tired; the honeymoon with their students has long been over; and they have not developed the positive relations in their classrooms that are critical when February and

March roll around. Such complaining doesn't help to solve the problem—and indeed, in my experience such statements usually have no basis in fact. Yet, as principals, we understand that perceptions can become reality. People who say, "This is the worst group of kids," soon start to believe it. Eventually, they start to treat them that way—and unfortunately, the students will start to behave accordingly.

Effective principals understand that one of the best ways to alter perceptions is to provide other perceptions. I'll give you an example from my first year as a principal.

I was hired in July. I had not met any of the teachers. When I started working regularly, teachers began to drop by the office. One by one, they complained about the student body: "The worst group of kids we've ever had." I was scared to death to start the school year. I remember thinking that these students must be really different from any other students in the world. I guess I was right; as I walked around the school and visited classes the first day, I realized that these students were so bad, they must have even skipped the first day!

Of course, they were there, and they were no different than the challenging students we all know. Yet I realized that the teachers' *perceptions* were an indication how they felt about the students and, ultimately, about teaching. If I could not change these perceptions, before long they would become reality. I pondered what to do.

About a month into the school year, I attended the annual state conference. One session, billed as a roundtable discussion, turned out to be a gripe session for principals, each relating their "biggest problem." I happened to sit next to the principal from a very wealthy school—we'll call it Country Club High. Well, I had always assumed that Country Club High could not possibly have problems. After all, at least partly because of their clientele, they always had outstanding test scores. Their sports teams were consistently winners, and salaries were the highest in the state. Imagine my surprise when their leader described his school's biggest problem as students "pantsing" drugs—putting drugs in their underwear so that they could not be searched. That really put things in perspective for me. I resolved to share this perspective with the teachers at my school.

At the next faculty meeting I told the story. When I reported that I sat next to the principal of Country Club High, the faculty gasped as if I'd met a famous movie star. Then I told them that students at the most prestigious school in the state routinely hid drugs in their underwear. My staff was speechless. Finally, I described the biggest problem at our school: The door to Dennis Newton's locker keeps sticking. Though they chuckled at my obvious attempt to downplay our issues, the teachers realized that many of the challenges posed by "the worst group of kids we've ever had" were closer to Dennis's locker-door problem then they were to "pantsing" drugs.

We are very fortunate to work in education; sometimes we just forget how blessed we are. By consistently filtering out the negatives that don't matter and sharing a positive attitude, we can create a much more successful school. Consciously or unconsciously, *we decide* the tone of our school.

6

Teach the Teachers

Certainly, the most important people in the school are the students. However, outstanding principals know that their primary role is to teach the teachers. The best way to provide an exceptional learning environment for students is to give them outstanding teachers. Great principals focus on students—by focusing on teachers.

Let's explore further a concept we mentioned in Chapter 2: Many factors influence the quality of a school, and changes in programs and procedures can have some impact, but when push comes to shove, the only ways a principal can improve a school are to hire better teachers or to improve the teachers who are already there.

In Chapter 7, we will discuss what effective principals do to hire outstanding teachers. Here, we address what the best principals do to improve the teachers they have.

Teachers Do the Best They Know How

I am convinced that most teachers do the best they know how. If we want them to do better, we must help them improve their skills and master new ones. And since teachers do the best they know how, we can expect that they will put new skills into practice. Let's break this down and see if it makes sense. We'll start with an area that affects all teachers: classroom management.

All teachers manage their classrooms the best they know how. Why am I so sure of this? Simply because good classroom management is in the teacher's best interest. What teacher does not want well-behaved students? Teachers who struggle with classroom management will eventually, if not immediately, become frustrated with their students' behavior. They may even come to resent the students. Surely, if they knew how to improve their students' behavior, they would do so. The best teachers may manage their classrooms well for the sake of the students, but all teachers will use good classroom management skills if they have them.

Recognizing this fact of human nature is an important first step toward bringing about change in your staff, not just in classroom management but in all aspects of teaching. If we assume that all teachers do the best they know how, we can switch our attention to improving what they know.

The Test Score Dilemma

As we mentioned in the last chapter, most of us have attended meetings and heard the clarion call, "Raise your test scores!" We may have heard it from the state department of education, from our own central office, or maybe even at a local school board meeting. I certainly have—and interestingly, at any of those meetings I would have bet my brown-bag lunch that everyone there was already doing their level best to achieve high test scores. Furthermore, no one likes to be told what to do; many people's instinct is to do the opposite. If we want people to do better, we must teach them how. During my first year as a classroom teacher, a colleague down the hall tended to repeat the same explanation or instructions over and over, raising the volume a little each time. Finally, she would cry out in exasperation, "I've told you at least a dozen times!" Every time I heard her say this, I thought to myself, "Now *there* is a slow learner." It's unrealistic—and frustrating—to expect someone to do better when they do not know a better way.

The Poor Lecturer

I would guess that everyone who has attended school has suffered (or dozed) through a boring lecture. Principals who drop in on an ineffective lecturer's classroom can tell in about two minutes that the students are completely uninterested. We often wonder, "Can't that teacher tell that the students are bored to death?" Most likely, the answer is No. Think about it: Students have been bored in that classroom for days, or months, or years; why would we think the teacher would notice today? The more important question is, "Can the teacher do anything about it?" Again, realistically, the answer is No. If the teacher could have identified the problem and figured out the solution, today's lecture would not have been boring. As principals, we must recognize that unless we show teachers a better way, they will probably never even attempt a different instructional practice.

Modeling Effective Interaction

Getting an "A" in a class means little in life if we cannot get along with others. Now, some students come from homes where two parents communicate and interact with each other in a positive manner. These students can watch adults resolve conflicts and develop ground rules. However, many of our students don't have this advantage. If we don't provide opportunities for them to observe adults working together successfully in our schools, they may never see this—and few careers reward workers who lack this important skill. We can't expect young people to learn this on their own; we must model it for them. This is one reason we have to develop ways for teachers to work together in our classrooms.

We Can't Teach from the Office

All principals face incredible demands on their time and energy. We're pulled in different directions every minute of the day. Less effective principals have dozens of reasons for not having time to visit classrooms daily, or at least weekly. Great principals have an equal number of demands placed on their time. They just do not let these reasons keep them from doing what matters most: improving teacher effectiveness in their school.

In many schools, a small number of teachers refer a disproportionate number of students to the principal's office. We could let these referrals keep us trapped there, reacting to problems. We could even argue that we cannot spend time in classrooms because of these few teachers. But unless we get out of our reactive mode and into an improvement mode, the problems that consume our days will never go away.

The most effective principals take the opposite approach. They find the time to get into these troubled teachers' classrooms and help build their skills. They make time to focus on instruction—by focusing on instruction. The more we can build the skills of our teachers, the less we are drained by reacting to the results of ineffective practices.

Highly effective principals understand their importance as role models. Of course, we all know that every adult in our school is a role model, one way or the other. However, the best principals know how to be role models for teachers. When teachers see us in their classrooms, they see how we expect them to interact with students. This is one of a principal's most significant jobs.

Get Teachers into Each Other's Classrooms

In my years as a principal, I often thought—and said—that the best teachers in my schools were much better teachers than I was. It would be foolish to pretend that I visited their classrooms just to improve their teaching. Quite the contrary: I learned from them, harvesting techniques and approaches that I could then model in other classrooms. My visits gave me the opportunity to support them—and to rejuvenate myself; in my best teachers' classrooms I remembered what school was all about. When I realized that others could learn from my superstar teachers too, getting other teachers into their classrooms became an essential tool. After all, who better to teach the teachers than those with the best skills?

One experience in particular taught me how important these learning opportunities can be. A school where I was principal received a grant to establish a student writing lab. Funds were included to staff the lab with writing specialists, one in the morning and another in the afternoon. Because this was not specifically tied to a particular class, we had to find a way to train every student to use the new equipment and software. We decided to have all the social studies teachers bring their students to the lab for three consecutive days, staying while the writing specialist led the training. Though I didn't say so, I selected social studies because some of those teachers were not among our most effective. One in particular was legendary for sitting behind his desk most of the time while his students did repetitive worksheets or answered questions from the dry history textbook.

Since the training was new, I dropped in regularly to observe. The morning writing specialist was a phenomenal teacher whom all the students admired. I happened into the lab when Mrs. Dynamite was leading the training for the legendary Mr. Doldrum's class. Not surprisingly, he took his usual position—wedged behind the desk in the computer lab.

I had visited Mrs. Dynamite's classes often, so her teaching style was familiar. When she observed the students at work, she would walk behind them, looking over their shoulders with her hands clasped behind her back. Twice more that morning, I looked in at the same scene—Mrs. Dynamite walking around with her hands behind her back, Mr. Doldrum parked behind the desk. But just two days later, it was a very different story.

I found Mrs. Dynamite interacting with students as she usually did, but Mr. Doldrum was not at his customary post. At first, I thought he must have slipped out of the room—but then a movement in the far corner caught my eye. There stood Mr. Doldrum—looking over a student's shoulder, hands clasped behind his back! At that moment, I realized that he barricaded himself behind his desk only because he did not know what else to do.

We worked together for the next three years, and I rarely saw him seated at his desk. Instead, he was on his feet, making the rounds, assisting students as they worked. Now, I could have badgered him for months on end to change his teaching style, and it is unlikely that he would have tried it—except possibly when I came into his room. But when he had the opportunity to observe a tremendously effective teacher, he emulated her behavior on his own. It was a lesson I never forgot.

One caution: It's important not to put the best teachers on a pedestal or single them out as examples for others. A more diplomatic—and more effective—approach is to frame the observations as a two-way street, an interaction between peers. For example, if Mrs. Jones is an outstanding teacher and Mr. Smith is less skilled, you would want them to observe in each other's rooms so that they can build a relationship. Otherwise, less effective teachers may work hard *not* to learn anything from the other teacher.

The Talent Exchange

The simplest approach is to start with your two points of least resistance: your best teachers and your new teachers. During the interview process, ask candidates what they would think about going into other teachers' classrooms on several occasions during their first couple of years. You should get a positive response—at least from those who want the job. And if you toss this idea out to your faculty, especially one-on-one, your best teachers are likely to be the first to volunteer. Now you can arrange for the new teachers to visit these best teachers' classrooms, and for the teacher volunteers to observe the new teachers. Obviously the new people will learn plenty, and your skilled teachers can support the "new kids on the block"— and in my experience, they learn a great deal from the interaction as well.

Gradually, you can expand this network. For example, have all third-grade teachers go into each other's rooms; then have first-grade teachers visit second grade, and vice versa. At the middle school level, teachers on a team can observe each other; follow this with visits between teams and grade levels. Create a wonderful opportunity to involve related arts by having core subject teacher and related arts teachers do individual visitations. At the high school level, the new teacher–best teacher exchange can lead to observations within and eventually across departments.

What do you do with the hesitant teachers? At first, nothing. Start where you can; if even just two teachers participate, your school is better off. Don't let those who drag their feet keep you from making a difference. As the number of teachers involved grows, peer pressure may have an effect; but even if some never participate, the rest will benefit. Those who overcome their reluctance are likely to be rewarded with a new sense of trust in their colleagues.

This collaboration among classroom teachers is one of the most basic and effective ways to improve instruction. Remember, our goal is to help all teachers be as good as our best teachers. A logical place to start is to give everyone a chance to observe and learn from quality. When we use our most effective teachers as positive role models, we multiply their productivity and help others maximize their talents. What's more, we raise the level of respect that other staff members have for our best teachers, which in turn enhances their influence throughout the school.

One of the great joys of being a principal is observing your best teachers in action. Share the wealth!

7

Hire Great Teachers

Chapter 6 focused on one of the basic ways to improve your school: by improving the teachers you have. This chapter addresses the other key component: hiring better teachers. A principal's single most precious commodity is an opening in the teaching staff. The quickest way to improve your school is to hire great teachers at every opportunity. Just as the only way to improve your average grade is to turn in a better-than-your-average assignment each time, the most significant way to rapidly improve a school is to add teachers who are better than the ones who leave. Great principals know this and work diligently to hire the best possible teachers.

The Great Principal's Goal

Some principals look for candidates who are a good match—teachers who will fit in and become like their school. Great principals have a different goal: to have the school become more like the new teacher. If this is not our goal and our outcome, then we are hiring the wrong people. It's simply impossible to improve a school by hiring people who fit right in with its average teachers.

Once we have hired dynamic new teachers, it's tempting to wonder how to spread their energy and excitement to the other teachers. Our first challenge, however, is to keep the new teachers enthusiastic. Think about it: Most teachers are full of energy

43

when they first start out. If all of them could sustain that drive, we wouldn't be working so hard to improve the teachers we have. Effective principals have learned that although maintaining a new teacher's level of energy is a challenge, at least momentum is on their side; by contrast, restoring the enthusiasm of a jaded teacher can be like pushing stones uphill. Great principals hire dynamic teachers and strive to keep them that way.

Just imagine how quickly your faculty and your school will improve if each new teacher you hire is your best teacher! Now let's look at the potential impact of your hiring decisions on others in the school.

Wanted: Leaders!

Astonishingly, many principals are willing to settle for a *good* teacher. The upside of this is that when other principals settle for *good,* great principals can hire the exceptional. What do great principals look for? They don't want just a *good* third-grade teacher or science instructor, or even just a *great* third-grade teacher or science instructor. Great principals look for the teachers who will be exceptional in the classroom; but more than that, they look for those who will be influential in the school. I never wanted to settle for teachers who could lead their students well; I sought teachers who could lead their peers. After all, I wanted my school to become more like the best teachers I hire; it wouldn't hurt to have their help.

We've seen the importance of understanding *who is the variable.* Likewise, we need to understand which qualities distinguish the great teachers from the good ones. We can start by identifying *what does not matter.*

Hire for Talent

I once had a colleague who would hire only teachers with their master's degree. I welcomed him as my main competitor in the hiring process, because he left me with carte blanche for all the other candidates—*and* I could still choose from the pool of candidates with advanced degrees. I'm not saying that a person's level of education is never a positive indicator (after all, I teach in a graduate program!)—but we all know people with advanced degrees who are not good teachers, and the lack of an advanced degree doesn't keep a teacher from being effective. The outstanding teacher who is one class short of a master's degree will not be a much stronger candidate when that arbitrary standard is met. The essential variable in hiring is the talent level of the teacher.

I define "talent" broadly. If intelligence were the only factor, we could recruit at the local Mensa meeting and reduce the paperwork to an IQ test and a contract. To me, talent means the total package: love of students, bright mind, positive attitude, congenial personality, great work ethic, leadership skills, charisma. I realize that we can't always find a candidate with all these qualities, but I believe we should keep the list at the forefront when we hire. Otherwise, we tend to make decisions based on factors that really won't matter in the long run.

It's fascinating to me that the qualities I define as talent are often more inherent than learned. As we saw in the previous chapter, skills can be improved; I'd rather start with someone who has a jarful of talent and a thimbleful of technique than the other way around. Think about your very best teachers. How effective do you think they were their first year of teaching? Even their first day? If you ask them, they may say they were terrible, but I find that high achievers hold themselves to very high standards. I'd bet that someone who brings that much talent to the table probably was pretty darn good starting from day one (and better by day three). By the same token, I doubt that any teacher experiences a sharp upturn in ability on commencement day of an advanced degree program.

Our best teachers are our best teachers. It's that simple. If we move our best teacher from the fifth-grade classroom to the first-grade classroom, we still have an effective teacher. Now, we might choose not to make that transfer; the teacher might be reluctant, or we might need leadership at the upper elementary level. Nevertheless, we could expect the transfer to work out well. On the other hand, if we move our least effective high-school math teacher to a different grade level, will we have an instant superstar? Of course not. This doesn't mean that "fit" doesn't matter. But if we hire highly talented people, they will thrive wherever we put them and will help make our school better. Hiring for talent is sure to pay off in the long run.

Experience Is Not the Best Teacher; the Best Teacher Is the Best Teacher

Amazingly, many principals feel that experience is the most important trait when hiring a new staff member. Well, I suppose that could be a factor—as long as it's great experience. But rank your own faculty from most effective to least effective; then note how many years of experience each has. Unless these two lists correlate perfectly, something else matters more than experience. (And if they do correlate perfectly, it's possible that whoever hired the veterans did a much better job than whoever chose the newer folks.) Of one thing I can assure you: If two teachers have different experience levels and different talent levels, the one with more talent will be better in the long run— and most likely in the middle run, and probably in the short run.

Let's say you hire two new teachers at a middle school. One has average talent—about 6.5 on a one-to-ten scale—and 12 years of experience; the other is a brand-new teacher with a talent level of 9. Picture the first days of school (when experience should matter most). Ms. Oldhand takes attendance the way she has for 12 years; roll call is uneventful, maybe even a little boring. Ms. Rookie struggles a little taking roll. She realizes that it took too long, and the kids got a little squirrelly.

Fast-forward one week. Ms. Oldhand calls the roll as she has done more than a thousand times. The kids still respond, but routine has set in. Meanwhile, Ms. Rookie has figured out a way to take attendance with a mini–Quiz Bowl. The kids are there on time, leaning forward in their seats.

Fast-forward again, and again. In about a month, Ms. Oldhand's students are starting to shut down during roll call. By the end of the semester, they may even be somewhat disrespectful. Some might even arrive a little late because they know the first three minutes are pretty irrelevant. Ms. Rookie's kids, on the other hand, get there early. She has decided to choose a student to emcee the Quiz Bowl each day, and those who are not in their seats on time miss out on this honor.

Now, you might object that this wouldn't happen quite so quickly. Sure, with an average veteran teacher the start-of-the-year excitement may last six weeks or more. And the new teacher might not have the Quiz Bowl in place until the start of the second year. However, my real point is that one of these teachers will predictably improve. More than that, one will make a difference in your school. Fast-forward three years: Five teachers use Quiz-Bowl roll call, and three of them structure it around state standards. Student test scores improve. You're named National Principal of the Year and Oprah invites you as a special guest. (Well . . . maybe at least your school improves!)

I'd like to share another telling example. The week before her first year at a school, an administrator friend had a last-minute special education opening in her behavioral disorders classroom—a principal's worst nightmare. She called me to ask if I knew of any candidates. By chance, I knew an exceptionally talented teacher who was moving to that town. (We'll call her Miss Johnson.) She was certified in special education, though I was not sure of the area. I also knew that my friend was inheriting a challenging faculty, and I viewed Miss Johnson as a good team player and an asset to school improvement efforts.

A few weeks later I saw my friend at the state conference and asked her how Miss Johnson was doing. She said she had not hired her. I was surprised, but asked how she filled the position. Well, she was concerned because Miss Johnson would have had to get a temporary license, and another applicant had the right certification and a few years of experience. To make a long story short, she hired the other teacher. By the end of the year, the new teacher had joined the group of griping staff members, and my friend chose to let her go. Interestingly, the following year she recruited Miss Johnson, who has helped the school become one of the best in the state.

One final example involves technology. Many schools and districts have adopted school-wide or district-wide technology programs. Some programs manage attendance records or grade reporting; others serve instructional purposes. Some leaders seek new hires who can hit the ground running with these programs. I disagree. I believe that talented candidates will quickly be up to speed on anything you currently have, but more importantly, they will become the frontrunners on anything you eventually get. They may not know the software on day one, but give them a weekend and they will master it; give them a month and they could train others. After a year, they will be eager for whatever new stuff you bring in. Remember, you don't want your new employees just to fit into your school; you want to hire the best, and have your school become like them.

There Is No Pecking Order

Exceptional principals consistently value people because they do the right thing for students and for the school, not merely because of seniority or other arbitrary factors. Of course, we recognize and value our senior staff members; if we fail to do this, we can quickly lose credibility. But effective leaders base their decisions on each individual's effectiveness and contributions. If we have to wait for new faculty to become veterans before making full use of their talents and gifts, they may well let their efforts flag, confine their energies to their classrooms, or go somewhere else where they can make a difference. There must be no pecking order in our schools.

It may seem that the best place to establish this attitude is among our existing staff; we may want to forestall the intimidating word or glance a veteran might use to keep rookies in their place. However, I'm convinced that the place to start is with the new faculty, and the time to start is during the interview.

As a principal, before offering a job to a promising candidate, I would state my position clearly: "I am looking to add teachers who want to be part of the best school in the United States. I want new teachers to speak up at the very first faculty meeting if they so choose. If I did not welcome your ideas, I would not bring you on board. I value the people who work to make this school the best it can be. There is no pecking order here."

I have had teachers tell me several years later how empowering that original contact was, and how they never forgot its message.

Start Induction at the Interview

Often, we assume that the induction process for new teachers begins during the week before school opens. Yes, we can continue the induction process then, but we need to start induction during the interview itself.

As soon as you realize that the candidate you are interviewing is a strong prospect, begin to make your expectations clear. Your approach will vary, depending on the situation. Let's say you need someone to join your high-school science department, currently not your best group of teachers. The person you hire will end up next door to a habitual griper who typically arrives late, leaves early, and would like others to adopt the same "just barely enough is good enough" attitude. You can simply select your top candidate and hope for the best; or you can set the stage for the person you hire to do the right thing despite the prevailing dynamics. During the interview, you can ask, "Suppose the teacher in the next classroom liked to do as little as possible—for example, arriving late and leaving early—and wanted you to do the same. What would you do?"

Why do you ask these questions during the interview? You ask then because *you need to know.* You want potential teachers to look you in the eye and make a commitment. You also do it because *they need to know* what you expect of them. Then, as the school year progresses, you can remind your new teacher of your conversation: "Do you have any idea why I asked you that question about working next door to a minimalist?" You are on the same page about which colleagues they should choose as role models.

Of course, the same applies to professional relationships you want to encourage. You could ask a candidate something like, "Miss Smith, if you end up working here, what would you think about calling another third-grade teacher, say, Mrs. Jones, and asking about what she does to help her students get off to a positive start?" Now, Miss Smith wants a job, so she'll probably agree that this is a good idea. Beyond that, you have planted the thought in her mind that you think well of Mrs. Jones, paving the way for a good relationship between a new staff member and a dynamic role model.

Great teachers do this with a class; they set expectations early and then follow through. Likewise, any game is more fun to play if the rules are clear from the start and don't change in the middle of the contest. As we'll discuss later, effective principals establish expectations at the initial staff meeting and consistently follow through on them each day. Successful principals hire outstanding teachers to help them achieve their goals for the school.

8

Standardized Testing

As a writer, speaker, and professor, I do my best to stay focused on enduring issues in our schools. I care most about staff motivation, teacher morale, school culture and climate, and student behavior. These core issues have been central to our schools—all schools—for decades and will remain essential decades from now. Likewise, I tend to stay away from the hot issue of the day (or year, or decade). A recent example is the dramatic emphasis on school safety. In reaction to several tragedies, our school systems came under pressure—either as public outcries or as state mandates, handed down to principals through central office staff—to develop a "disaster plan" for each building.

Different schools reacted in different ways. Some principals placed the issue front and center. At the next faculty meeting, they asked for volunteers to be on a safety committee. Predictably, teachers hemmed and hawed until the two or three best teachers raised their hands. Again predictably, the committee worked very hard and developed a terrific disaster plan, complete with color-coded escape routes, tabbed references, community-wide contact people, and so on. The school was all set.

Four or five years from now, someone will stumble across that plan and realize that it is outdated: The counselor is different, several key contacts are gone, and even the physical plant

51

has changed. Future school staff may say the school was lucky not to have needed the disaster plan, or realize that in an actual emergency, common sense would prevail over any formal plan developed years ago. They may or may not update the plan; another hot issue is front and center now, and they are busy reacting to it. Other principals were able to step back and realize that even the best disaster plan, worked out in painstaking detail, would never cover all scenarios. Furthermore, they didn't want to burden their best teachers with this task. So they recruited a variety of teachers, including some solid veterans, to develop a basic plan, which they reviewed and handed in to the central office.

Effective principals don't let hot-button issues shift their focus from what really matters. A disaster plan, though valuable, is not the core of a school. The best principals spend their human resources carefully, aware of the limited value of many mandates from on high. With this context as the backdrop, I'm now going to tiptoe into the shark-infested pool of standardized testing.

Without Success, Tests Become the School

If you want to hear an emotional debate, bring up politics or religion—but if you overhear teachers arguing about one of these mainstream topics and want to escalate the battle, ask them to share their views on standardized testing. Though mandated testing has been around in some states for decades, it is still evolving everywhere. The tests change, testing dates change, different grade levels are included or excluded, open-ended assessments are on the horizon. And each change in state or federal testing requirements brings another opportunity to discuss the merits of that change and of testing in general.

Like everyone else, principals have different personal viewpoints on standardized testing. Yet, no matter what our beliefs, we must deal with the reality of standardized tests. How do we go about it?

First of all, we must move away from debating the merits of standardized testing. Strongly held personal beliefs tend to

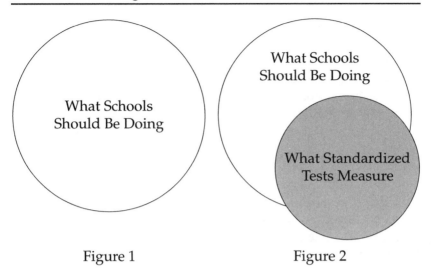

Figure 1   Figure 2

dominate that debate. We must shift our focus away from beliefs and center on behaviors. The following chapter explores this in more depth, but the concept applies directly to the testing issue that consumes so much attention today. If we can agree on behaviors, our school and our district can move forward in harmony regardless of our personal feelings. Like two parents with differing beliefs on discipline, we can work toward consensus on the consistent *behaviors* that are essential for success.

If we brought together all our different constituent groups—teachers, parents, administrators, board members, students, community representatives—we might be surprised to discover how much we agree on. Here's an exercise to share with your staff. Let's imagine that we ask all these people, either collectively or individually, a couple of key questions.

The first and most important question is this: *What should our schools be doing?* I believe we will find an affirming overlap of answers. Though some may want more emphasis on math or physical education, arts or technology, our different constituent groups generally agree on what schools should be doing. We can represent this area of agreement as one big circle, shown in Figure 1.

Now, let's ask the same groups—again either collectively or individually—question number two: *What do standardized tests measure?* Though there are explicit listings of most state test standards, people still have a variety of beliefs about what they actually measure. Whatever their beliefs are, let's represent them in a smaller circle, shown with the larger circle in Figure 2.

Ask your staff whether they feel that, on the whole, these two circles depict their personal views regarding the relationship between what schools should be doing and what standardized tests measure. Before they respond, you might note that some may think the second circle, or the overlap between the two, should be larger (or smaller). Don't get into a hairsplitting contest. Instead, ask whether they agree that the first circle is the core of your school.

Next comes the essential step: shifting the focus from views and beliefs to behaviors. Express to the faculty your conviction that no matter how we personally see the relationship between the small circle and the large circle, we as a school must achieve success within the smaller circle or it will become our big circle (Figure 3)—and no one in this school wants that.

This approach gives our most resistant test opponents a reason to become strong test result advocates. Even the teacher

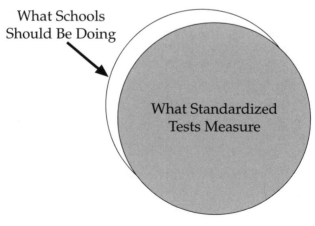

Figure 3

who least believes in standardized testing now has an incentive to work toward student success in this area. We can now center on the same behaviors, working toward the same goal *regardless of our beliefs*. As leaders, we too can maintain our personal beliefs about the merits of testing while we move our school toward success.

Standardized tests measure only a part of what schools should be doing. Effective leaders focus on the behaviors that lead to success, not the beliefs that stand in the way of it. Effective principals don't let standardized tests take over the entire school.

Effective Principals Keep Testing in Perspective

In a study of principals who led schools that exceeded expectations on standardized tests (Turner 2002), the perspectives of the principals were very refreshing. These principals did not believe in the value of testing more than others; they just understood the importance of test results to others. They were fully aware that success on standardized tests brought their school greater autonomy to do what they believed was best for students. These principals also understood how the tests and state standards could provide a powerful backdrop for improving and aligning curriculum. Before state-mandated testing, for many teachers the textbook was their curriculum. The state standards forced educators to shift the focus to what our curriculum was and helped us center on the real issue of student learning.

Interestingly, however, the more effective principals in the study described student achievement in a much broader sense than did principals whose schools underachieved on standardized tests. No matter what the socioeconomic background, schools that performed poorly defined student achievement only in terms of test scores. Effective principals (whose schools had equally diverse clientele) and their teachers mentioned test scores, but they also listed student social skills, self-worth, behavior, responsibility, involvement in

school, and other such characteristics as important compo-
nents of student achievement.

The more effective principals were also aware of the risk of
making state standards the center of the school. If your school's
core rests on state standards, then you had better hope that the
standards never change, because if they do, you have lost the
core of your school. Instead, every decision should rest on
doing what is best for students. Then when new mandates and
programs come into play, you can examine how they fit into
what you are already doing that is best for the students.

9

Focus on Behavior, Then Focus on Beliefs

In some ways, this chapter may seem like a contradiction. I firmly believe that effective principals can, and should, instill their values and beliefs at the heart of their schools. (As a matter of fact, over time even a less effective principal's beliefs can permeate the school.) However, one hallmark of effective leaders is what they do when not everyone shares their beliefs.

Effective principals recognize the difficulty of changing a person's lifelong beliefs. What's more, they know that sometimes what really matters is not beliefs, but behavior. In other cases, a change in behavior naturally leads to a change in beliefs. Therefore, effective principals focus on behaviors, then on beliefs.

In Chapter 4, I mentioned my often-repeated statement to my teachers: "You don't have to like the students, you just have to act as if you like them." The same applies to student behavior. High-school teachers may have one kind of problem if students think a particular class is boring—but they have a greater problem when students *act* as if a class is boring (whether it actually is or not). In an ineffective teacher's class, most students wish they were somewhere else. However, the students everyone loves—the teacher-pleasers—still seem glad to be there, at least compared to many of the others. Like the best teachers, they show an interest in every person and every situation they encounter.

The opposite is also true. I once worked with a teacher whose mannerisms sent very negative messages. For example, if something happened that she didn't like, she would put her hands on her hips and sigh. After working with her for a while, I realized that her negative body language was more a matter of habit than an expression of contempt. But others were offended; students in particular concluded that she didn't like them. When I shared these thoughts with the teacher, she was aghast. She really liked teaching and her students—but because her behavior didn't reflect this, she struggled much more with student relations than her abilities and efforts warranted. Once she became aware of and changed her behavior, she became more effective with her students.

Now, if I had focused on why she didn't like teaching or her students, we never would have moved forward. In any case, the issue wasn't her beliefs, but her behavior. No matter how she felt about the students, it was essential that she treat them in an appropriate manner. Whether or not her beliefs were altered, I do not know. But I can assure you that her behaviors were because I, like her students, could see the difference.

Understanding Incentives

In an ideal world, everyone in our school would make every decision based on what is best for the students. And many do—especially our most effective teachers. However, all teachers also share the human trait of acting in their own best interests. In the classroom, as in life, they want to do what works for them. As we emphasized in Chapter 6, teachers generally do the best they know how. Likewise, once people know a better way, they are likely to use it. Well then, why don't all teachers simply change their behaviors when we present a new approach?

The greatest impediment to change is fear, especially fear of the unknown. Some people instinctively recognize a better idea, a more effective technique, a change worth making, but others do not. Even if a new approach is guaranteed to work, the transition is scary. It may seem safer to cling to familiar practices, even if they don't work very well at all.

We can't convince people to change simply by urging them to adopt our beliefs. However, if we center our efforts on getting staff members to try a new approach, they may find that it actually works for them. I'd like to share some examples.

Let's Call Those Parents

All principals would like their teachers to initiate contact with parents. Teachers who do this—and do it effectively—see the rewards; often, talking with parents leads to improved student behavior or effort. Furthermore, teachers who initiate communication when it is needed reduce the chance that they will receive unpleasant calls from concerned or angry parents. Calling parents sooner rather than later avoids the "Why didn't I know?" response that makes teachers feel defensive. Thus, calling parents first makes sense to many staff members in our schools.

Even in schools where most teachers contact parents regularly, a few may not. Many are reluctant because their previous experiences with parents have been negative—perhaps because they have waited until concerned parents make the initial contact. As a result, many teachers (and principals!) build up a wall of resistance to initiating calls to parents.

We could spend time trying to convince, argue, or cajole these reluctant teachers into *believing* us when we say calling parents will work. On the other hand, what we really want is to change their behavior. We want teachers to call and ask for a parent's help before a small problem becomes a big problem. This might eventually lead them to change their beliefs—but even if it doesn't (and it may be impossible or irrelevant to know), the altered behavior will be enough to improve parent-teacher relations and, through that, improve our school.

However, some teachers may hesitate to call parents because they do not know what to say. If we do not help them learn what to say, it's unrealistic to expect them to want to place those awkward calls.

In the book *Dealing with Difficult Parents (And with Parents in Difficult Situations)* (Whitaker and Fiore 2001), a discussion gives teachers the language to initiate contact with parents when a child's behavior begins to show an inappropriate pattern (such as coming to class unprepared or bullying on the playground). When we teach our faculty what specific statements to use, we empower them and can reasonably expect them to make calls to parents. Once they do call parents in an appropriate manner, they will realize that this really does bring about changes in the students' behavior—changes that help the teacher. When teachers change their behavior and experience positive results, they are likely to continue and even expand their contact with parents.

Let's Praise Those Students

As we noted in Chapter 4, effective principals believe in the power of praise. As long as we praise correctly (Bissell), we cannot praise too much. Not all teachers share this belief. Will preaching to them about the value of praise change their minds? Probably not. Instead, we must teach them the techniques of appropriate praise and get them to try it. Once teachers begin to praise students, two things happen: The students improve their behavior, and the teachers feel better too. When teachers see positive results in their own classrooms, they see that praising students is in their own best interest. Have we changed their beliefs about the power of praise? Perhaps. At least now they know praise works for them—and that works just fine for us.

Let's Improve Those Instructional Practices

Think about the struggle to introduce team teaching in a middle school or block scheduling in a high school. Most likely, a few teachers see the change as "best for the students" and are ready to move forward. What gives them this confidence? Perhaps they are effective with students in general and comfortable in admitting mistakes. Almost everything works for them, so they don't fear change. Others are not so quick to join in. The way things are now may not be great, but it's familiar and safe—they know how it works. They may have tried a new approach in the past and lacked the personality or skills to pull it off. They're not convinced that this change is a good idea.

In this situation, effective leaders don't waste their time or energy trying to persuade everyone that the new system will work better than the old. Instead, they provide a scaffolding of procedures and techniques that helps the timid to feel secure. They structure the change so that the reluctant do not have the option to balk or turn back. They focus on behaviors, not beliefs.

I have seen industrial arts teachers who would not even consider moving from making birdhouses to using the industrial technology more appropriate to the times. No amount of lobbying persuaded them to change their practices. However, once the old equipment was trucked away and computer workstations were installed, their interest in being trained went up considerably—and once they had to try the new approach, they believed in it.

Of course, effective principals maintain a professional respect for others' beliefs. And at times, they still encourage, cajole, persuade, and lobby their teachers to change their beliefs. But in certain situations, beliefs are irrelevant; what really matters is behavior. In other situations, a change in behavior paves the way for a change in beliefs. In these situations, effective principals focus on behaviors, not on beliefs.

10

Loyal to Whom?

We often hear of leaders encouraging, expecting, or even demanding loyalty. This is not a new concept; all leaders—in the field of education and elsewhere—understand that loyalty is important. Effective principals expect loyalty from their employees; so do their less effective colleagues.

In this book, however, I focus on the differences between outstanding principals and others. The important question here is not whether school leaders expect loyalty. The important question is, "Loyalty to whom?"

Loyalty to the Students

All principals would like their staff members to be loyal to them. Some principals expect it; some less effective principals "demand" it (whatever that means). The most effective principals also insist on loyalty—to the *students*.

Great principals believe that if you are loyal to the students, you are loyal to the principal. What do they mean by loyalty? To a great principal, loyalty means making decisions based on what is best *for the student*—but more than that: what is best *for all the students*.

What Is Best for the Student(s)?

Teachers and principals faced with decisions about disciplinary matters often hear the question, "What is best for the student?" (Should I send her to the office? Should we suspend him from school? What consequence is best for that individual?) This is a good question to ask, but it should not be raised in isolation. Instead, it should always be coupled with the parallel one: "What is best *for this student* and what is best *for all the students*?"

Sadly, sometimes we must remove a student from a classroom or the school, not because it is best for that student, but because it is best for all the other students. If we think too narrowly, we make our decision based on one child (possibly the one child who is benefiting least from the class) at the expense of the other students who are affected by that one individual.

Here's another way to look at the same question. We can ask what is best for the student, but we also need to ponder what is best for the school. Otherwise, we focus on the one student who has chosen to be disruptive, ignoring the rest. Certainly, we should consider the best options for the troubled child—but we must always also consider the best options for all the young people in our classrooms and schools.

The same principle applies to every adult in our building. Every person must consistently ask, "What is best for the students?" Effective principals expect teachers to place the needs of their students ahead of their own personal desires, and they expect no less of themselves. Otherwise, we shift our focus— the core of our school—from the students to ourselves.

What Is Best for the School?

Principals must apply these same guidelines in dealing with staff members. When we make decisions, we can ask, "What is best for this teacher?" Should I assign her to a different grade level or a larger class? Should I send him to the workshop on effective communication skills? Should I speak with him about his classroom management style? However, we must ask this question in the larger context of what is best *for all the teachers* and what is best *for the school*.

This focus helps us to make the right decision, not necessarily the easy decision. When we hesitate to discipline a child or take up an issue with a teacher, it's easy to use the rationale, "I don't want to hurt their feelings," when it is really our own feelings that we want to protect.

If we hire less effective teachers because we think they will be more loyal to us, we miss an opportunity to improve our school. Talented teachers are often strong-willed. At times they will challenge our decisions. At times they will strongly oppose them. However, if their focus is consistently on the students, perhaps they are right. In fact, I have always believed that no matter how much two people disagree, if both consistently make their decisions based on what is best for students, then they are both right.

This kind of loyalty helps us keep our compass set on "true north"—maximizing what we can do for the young learners in our schools. All principals would like their teachers to be loyal to them. Effective principals expect their teachers to be loyal to their students. Great principals are loyal to their students, to their teachers, and to the school.

11

Base Every Decision on Your Best Teachers

Every leader makes decisions that will be controversial. And every principal has teachers who gripe and complain, teachers who drag their feet, and teachers who do their jobs well and embrace change. One of the most critical differences between effective principals and other principals is where they place their focus when they make tough decisions. The best principals base every decision on their best teachers. This may seem counter-intuitive; after all, traditional thinking says "teach to the middle." But if we want our schools to work better, we will find ways to focus on our best teachers.

Al Burr (1993) describes three kinds of teachers: superstars, backbones, and mediocres. Our best teachers typically fall into the superstar category. Here are some quick guidelines as we think of teachers who are superstars:

♦ Former students remember them as their best teachers.

♦ Parents regularly request these teachers for their children.

♦ Their peers respect these teachers.

♦ If they left your school, you probably would not be able to hire other teachers as good to replace them.

Our superstars are the cream of the crop—the top five to ten percent of our staff members. We may have only one or two teachers in this category; if we are lucky, we have as many as ten or twelve. The most effective principals understand that their school will go as far as their best teachers take it. They value their superstars.

What Will My Best Teachers Think?

Before making any decision or attempting to bring about any change, effective principals ask themselves one central question: "What will my best teachers think?" This does not mean that effective principals do not consider views from anyone else; but they *always* consider what their best teachers will think.

In a study of more effective and less effective middle school principals, Whitaker (1993) found three critical hallmarks of the best principals. One was that they routinely consulted informal teacher leaders for input before they ever made a decision. Why? Well, ask yourself these two questions:

+ If my best teachers don't think something is a good idea, what are the chances that the rest of the faculty will accept it?

+ If my best teachers don't think something is a good idea, what are the chances that it is a good idea?

As a principal, I regularly bounced ideas off a handful of my key staff members before I made a decision. Their acceptance was an important step toward implementation of any change.

Happily, we don't have to guess what our best teachers will think of an idea; we can ask them. Our superstars will tell us the truth in a way that we can accept. Furthermore, they will keep our conversations confidential; if they were habitual gossipers, their peers would not respect them so highly.

Our best teachers also have a school-wide vision. Some teachers tend toward tunnel vision, focusing on their own programs.

(This is not a criticism at all; such an approach is only human nature.) However, our superstars understand their role and program in a much larger context. Though they can lobby skillfully for their own programs and classrooms, they always have an understanding and awareness of the other facets of a school and district. Thus, their perspective on any decisions we make can be very beneficial to us as leaders.

This is not to exclude input from everyone else. That is important also, but maybe for a different reason. We ask for input from the vast majority of our faculty so they will feel a part of the decisions. We ask for input from our superstars so we will make the best decisions.

The most effective principals have the confidence to seek input in advance and feedback after the fact. Interestingly, less effective principals are less eager to have these superstar teachers in their schools. Every time they make a decision, they are conscious that the superstars are watching. When we lack confidence in ourselves, we are uncomfortable having outstanding colleagues around. But if we can swallow our pride and ask them in advance when appropriate (and after the fact when that is our only option), all of us can improve our skills and practice something that the best principals consistently do.

Implementing a New Idea

Principals use many strategies to facilitate change in their schools. A common strategy is to send groups of teachers to visit other schools where new ideas and practices are in place and thriving. Of course, this can be productive—but think how much more productive it would be to have these same positive examples in our own school. Well, the superstars are the best place to start fostering that internal expertise. They have already earned the respect of their peers, and the new ideas they implement are very likely to work. When we can draw on role models in our own school, the chances of expanding acceptance and implementation grow exponentially.

Most principals think they should base their decisions and focus their time and energy on their "backbone" teachers (the middle eighty to ninety percent of the faculty). They see this as the way to move their school forward. However, they are forgetting the power of peer pressure. Once the superstars move forward, the backbones will move with them. Even the staff members who fall in the category of "mediocres" tend to follow the crowd. The gripers, the complainers, the foot-draggers still want attention—and they can get attention only by being where others are.

Effective principals understand that the hardest teacher to move forward is the first one, not the last one. Less effective leaders focus on the their most resistant teachers. They look at a new program and think, "Mrs. Roadblock won't do it, so there is no reason to try." There is little chance of getting *everyone* on board if you can't get *one* person on board. You won't have cooperative learning in *all* your classrooms until at least one teacher in your school applies cooperative learning. Your best teachers are confident enough to take the risk of trying something new, and—even more important—they are talented and intuitive enough to make it work. As respected role models for other staff members in the school, your superstars lead the way.

Although great principals are aware that research is valuable, even essential, they do not require their best teachers to show research to support a new idea's effectiveness before trying it in their classrooms. Superstars tend to be highly innovative and creative; there may not be research on the new ideas that intrigue them. Instead, we should allow them to start small, in their own classrooms. The research can follow as we help expand the programs that work for our best teachers.

My Best Teachers Will Be "Fine" No Matter What

One of the ideas that I hear regularly from leaders is that they focus on their backbone or mediocre teachers because their best teachers "will be fine anyhow." Well, I agree that your superstars will be fine if you ignore them—but if your best teachers are only fine, they are no longer great.

Sure, these highly talented individuals will be fine on their own. The atmosphere in their classrooms will remain positive;

they will always treat their students with dignity and their colleagues with respect. But when we shift our focus away from what our superstars most need, we slowly (or maybe not so slowly) disenfranchise them. They may not rebel publicly, at least for a long time. But what happens may be even sadder and more costly: We lose their voice in the school.

Think of it this way: Our superstars will always be effective teachers, but if we do not value their contributions, they will limit their influence to their individual classrooms. It's as if they close their door to the school—not physically, but emotionally. As principals, we need our superstars to influence their grade level, their team, their department, and the entire school. We can't afford to drain away the dedication of our most valuable staff members by focusing on the others. Let's take a look at a couple of all-too-common examples.

Hey, I Said *One* Box of Paper Clips!

Almost every school has a limited budget and limited supplies. We all need to pinch pennies wherever we can. However, when we do this by issuing orders and directives, we insult the good people who already follow the rules—and we have no effect on the others.

In the book *Dealing With Difficult Teachers* (1999), I gave the example of the copy machine with a sign above it stating, "Limit: 20 Copies!" The purpose, of course, is to keep certain people from overusing the copier. But what happens? Well, our high achievers take the message to heart. Remembering one occasion seven years ago when they made 23 copies, they wonder if they should reimburse the school. On the other hand, the folks who abuse the copy machine already know they shouldn't—but they do it anyway. They'll just ignore our sign, or add a string of zeros behind the 20, or take it down and make 28 copies of it! And even if we padlocked the copier, they would make up the difference in paper clips.

It's a mistake to focus on our least effective people, issuing broad directives because of one or two miscreants. At best, we make our superstars feel guilty; at worst, we insult them. They think, "Why are you talking to me about this? Why don't you talk to them?" And they're right; why are we talking to them? Instead, we need to be sensitive to and support them. After all, they are going to decide the success of our school.

If we don't know who's overusing the copier, we need to find out. If we do know, we need to speak to them directly. We might tell them to clear all copy requests through us. They may find a way to get around any restrictions, but at least we haven't insulted our best people.

The same rule applies when paperwork deadlines approach. Blanket statements like "Some teachers still need to turn grades in!" not only allow laggards to hide in anonymity, but also make your best teachers worry. Did they forget to turn in any grades? Did the secretary misplace their paperwork? Did the computer eat their effort marks? By asking, "What would my best teachers think?" we can foster, not detract from, the ownership that our superstars feel for us and the school.

The Principal's Pet

It's important not to put a superstar in the position of being seen as the "principal's pet." A superstar may in fact be our trusted advisor, but if other staff members perceive the relationship as favoritism, they may lose respect for, and even resent, the superstar. We must use discretion in asking for input and feedback. Our true superstars don't want to be singled out for special treatment in front of their peers. (Other teachers might, but they are not our most effective and respected staff members.)

This concept of centering on the best teachers may seem new and unfamiliar, yet it is one of the crucial differences between the best leaders and the rest of the leaders. Just as the top echelon of a sales force accounts for the majority of a company's sales, your key staff members do most of the work. Nurture the superstars you have, and work to cultivate others. Keep your superstars at the forefront when you make decisions. Your school will be better off—and your job will be more enjoyable!

12

In Every Situation, Ask Who Is Most Comfortable and Who Is Least Comfortable

All principals face the challenge of balancing rules and guidelines with those times when we need to make exceptions. This is especially true when it comes to behavior expectations for students. We can be concise, be clear, and communicate— but situations still arise when tough decisions are much more in shades of gray than we wish.

Likewise, all principals establish internal ground rules that reflect our core belief systems, even though it seems that at least some of the time other influences tread on them. This chapter presents one internal standard that supports effective leadership: When making decisions, ask, "Who is most comfortable and who is least comfortable in this situation?" This goes along with the guideline from Chapter 11, "Make every decision based on the best teachers."

Treat Everyone As If They Were Good

A friend of mine has made a good living—in fact, a fortune—by buying apartment buildings, fixing them up, and renting them out. Any time someone I know becomes successful doing something I could probably do, I'm intrigued to learn more about it. One night I asked what he does if he purchases a building with undesirable tenants living in one of the apartments. His response struck a chord: "If there are tenants I would rather not have, I just remodel their apartment. They're not used to living in a nice place, so they either start behaving as if they deserve to stay there or they become so uncomfortable that they move out."

The same phenomenon occurs in our schools: When people become uncomfortable, they change. As principals, we should be careful to make this work for us. We want the ones who are uncomfortable to change in a positive direction; we don't want to create an uncomfortable situation for our best teachers. Let's look at an example involving a faculty meeting.

If one of our less effective staff members continually brings up negative points and dominates the meeting, the best teachers will be uncomfortable. The less positive faculty members may actually enjoy it. If we lose our cool and react unprofessionally, our best teachers become even more uncomfortable and will distance themselves from us. But what if we handle the situation with aplomb? We might say, "I think that is a point worth pursuing. Let's talk about it later this week. I'm usually here by 6:30; pick a morning that works for you." Mr. Negativity has lost his audience (and will have to get up early if he wants to keep griping). The most positive staff members will gratefully align themselves on our side.

The same applies to students. We have all seen graffiti in bathroom stalls, in public places, and unfortunately sometimes in schools. In my visits to schools, I have seen some boys' restrooms with the doors removed from the stalls. When I inquired, I was told this was done to stop graffiti. Who became most uncomfortable? All the well-behaved students who have not been writing on the stalls but have lost their privacy. The perpetrators probably enjoy the attention. (And if we think about it, there are many worse places for people to write obscenities than inside a bathroom stall.)

We can apply the same principle to working with parents. I recently saw a memo sent home with all 800 students in a school. The note said:

> Dear Parents,
>   You MUST pick your child up promptly any time we have an away field trip and the field trip buses return after the regular buses have left! *If you do not,* your child could be placed in after-school daycare and you could be charged up to $2.00 an hour.

Now ask yourself: Out of 800 families, how many were that note actually written for? Probably three or four—ironically, the three or four least likely to read the note. This principal has insulted some 795 families because of a small minority of others. What's more, these three or four already knew they were supposed to pick up their children; they just didn't do it. The note addressed to the entire population actually allows them to be more comfortable. They can think to themselves, "There must be lots of us who don't pick up our children on time."

On the other hand, the rest of the folks are wondering, "What are you talking to me for?" The decision to send a note to everyone makes all the responsible parents uncomfortable in the hope of reaching a few. A more effective approach would be to call the small number of negligent parents—making *them* uncomfortable.

If you feel that some kind of general reminder is necessary, focus on the positive families and treat everyone as if they were good. A note could read:

> Dear Parents,
>   Thank you for your support in picking up your child promptly any time we have an away field trip and the field trip buses return after the regular buses have

left. This enables us to provide more educational opportunities for our students and provides a safer environment for all the young people in our schools. Thank you
for your efforts.

This message is just as effective a reminder to the small
number of parents who were not there to pick up their children.
The difference is that the note reinforces the good behavior; it
makes the prompt parents more comfortable and the late ones
uncomfortable.

I am not a big fan of notes and would not necessarily
encourage the second approach, but at the very least it allows
you to make the people who did what is right feel good. The
same thing is true with teachers. When grades are due, you can
send out a curt email or memo:

Reminder! All grades are due promptly at 3:30 p.m. this
afternoon.

That way you can bother the high achievers who have already
turned in their grades.
Or you could shift the focus:

Thanks so much to those of you who are turning in your
grades promptly. It makes the end of term much more
manageable for Mrs. Smith, our dynamic secretary.
Anything we can do to help her helps all of us. Thanks
again.

This approach can guide decisions in many areas. Think of
the teacher who punishes an entire class because of a few students' behavior. Maybe the misbehaving students feel some
level of discomfort, but certainly the most responsible students
are upset and have much less respect for the teacher. Teachers
who ask themselves, "How will my best students feel as a
result of my decision?" will probably take a different approach
to discipline.

Uncomfortable Feelings Make People
Change—One Way or Another

If a principal argues with a belligerent parent, who feels uncomfortable? Not the parent; hostile parents love to argue. It's their niche. That's one good reason never to argue with difficult people—they have a lot more practice at it! However, another reason is that part of our job as teachers is to teach people appropriate ways to behave, not just help them refine the inappropriate skills they already have in abundance.

No, it's the principal who argues with a parent who feels uncomfortable and is likely to avoid the parent. The parent actually feels empowered—free to go tell everyone how the principal acted, what was said, and how the argument ended. That parent will come back to the school ready for battle.

Reflect on the example—"Limit: 20 Copies!"—discussed in the last chapter. This approach does make some people uncomfortable—the ones who hold themselves to high standards. Your high achievers will feel affronted, and they will behave differently; they will be less enthusiastic about work and move away from the heart of the school.

On the other hand, this generalized approach has little or no impact on the people for whom it was intended. They already have managed to rationalize why they deserve to ignore the rules. If anything, now they spend even more time thinking about how to get away with something.

If applied consistently, the question "Who is most comfortable and who is least comfortable?" can bring clarity to our decision making. We are not painting on a blank canvas; we have outlines to follow. We may decide to do something that will make the least effective teachers uncomfortable, but at the very least, our decisions will not make our best teachers uncomfortable.

Effective principals find that this ground rule—make the people who do the right thing feel comfortable—works for them too. They feel more comfortable with their decision making!

Pay for Performance

I now work as professor at a university. Universities follow an interesting dynamic: Nobody is in charge of anybody. That is both good and bad. The good part is that no one is in charge of you. The bad part is that no one is in charge of anyone else. Though this may be a slight exaggeration, it is much more fact than fiction.

One trend in higher education is called "Pay for Performance." At our university, raises for faculty members are established by peer review. It's as if all of the principals in a district decided how much of a pay raise each of their peers should get, or the teachers in a school voted on individual salary increases for fellow teachers.

As you can imagine, this is a controversial process. Job performance at a university is nearly impossible to quantify. Feelings get hurt, emotions run high, and relations become strained. After the first year, a confidential survey was conducted to determine what the faculty thought about the program. I happened to run into the university president—a man I hold in high regard—just after he received the results. He was very interested in reviewing the feedback on this innovative program.

I agreed with the president that the information could be valuable. However, I added that the perspectives of the entire faculty were not the decisive factor. He asked what I meant. I said that he should identify the five percent of the faculty whom he hoped would feel rewarded by pay for performance. If his very best employees felt reinforced, then the perspectives of the others might be helpful. But if they did not, then the program was not worthwhile—no matter what the others thought.

As it happened, the survey showed that about one third liked the program, one third were neutral, and one third did not like it. Well, it sure depends which third thought what, doesn't it? If the "worst" third of the faculty is uncomfortable with the program, there may be reason to consider making it permanent. But even if only five percent of the faculty disapprove, if that five percent represent the cream of the crop, then it is critical to revisit the entire concept. What really matters is what the best people think.

Effective principals continually ask themselves who is most comfortable and who is least comfortable with each decision they make. When we face a challenging decision, we'll feel less alone if we ask ourselves, "What will my best teachers think?" And we'll feel even less alone if we go to our superstars and ask them what they think.

13

Understand High Achievers

One of a principal's greatest challenges is to work success-fully with high achievers. Our high achievers do so much of the work within a school; if we do not work with them effectively, we will lose their valuable contributions, which often cannot be replaced. Effective principals understand these key people, are sensitive to their needs, and maximize their ability.

Ignore Minor Errors

In a study examining differences between more effective and less effective principals, Doug Fiore (2000) determined that one significant variation is that the very best leaders ignore minor errors. Though this finding was not limited to how they treat high achievers, we can see how it would readily come into play. High achievers hold themselves to very high standards. They expect to succeed at everything they do and work exceed-ingly hard to do so. That is one reason they are so good.

When high achievers have their shortcomings pointed out by someone else, they emotionally deflate. They are used to expecting tremendous things of themselves and they hate to let others down. If we point out minor flaws in their achievements, they take fewer risks and keep their successes more private.

This is just the opposite of what we want our best role models to do. We want their work to shine as an example and inspiration to others.

The Fiore study also pointed out that if principals harp on minor errors, the faculty shies away from contact or interaction with them. The less effective the principal, the greater the likelihood that teachers will describe that leader's comments as consistently negative. For the sake of our own self-worth, we tend to stay away from someone who regularly points out our mistakes.

A friend of mine is a truly outstanding principal, one of the best in the country. When a new superintendent arrived in his district, my friend was eager for him to visit his school. We all like to show off what we are most proud of (that is why we carry our children's pictures in our wallet or purse!), and he was no exception. His faculty and staff had done some outstanding things and he was proud to have others see them.

Not long after the new superintendent started work, he arranged to spend a morning in my friend's school, walking around and observing in the classrooms. The principal was ecstatic. This was great. The new superintendent was going to see all of the wonderful things taking place in his school.

Well, the superintendent stopped by the office and then spent a couple of hours dropping into classrooms. The principal could not wait to hear the feedback. Finally, the moment arrived; the superintendent sat down in the principal's office. He asked the name of the teacher who had the end room in the first hallway. That was good news to the principal, because it was Mr. Martin, a second-year teacher and one of his best. The principal happily related how he had hired Mr. Martin away from another school, what innovative ideas Mr. Martin had brought to the building, and what a great role model he was for the students. Yes indeed, he was quite pleased with Mr. Martin and with himself at that point in time.

However, the superintendent then said that the reason he asked was that Mr. Martin had been using the overhead projector—and a couple of times, for a second or two, his hand obscured the screen. Yikes! Talk about nitpicking!

We can all imagine how this felt to the principal. With so many wonderful things going on, the district leader's first visit to the school was summed up in the most trivial of criticisms. Not only was it hurtful, but also it took away any incentive to welcome the superintendent for another visit. And more than that, it put a damper on the principal's efforts. He is still effective in his school, but he has pulled back; his accomplishments no longer have district-wide impact. He hopes no one else, especially his supervisor, finds out about them.

The same thing happens to high-achieving teachers when we do not handle them appropriately. High achievers put so much of themselves into what they do that any criticism, no matter how minor, can become a personal affront. After all, no one really believes there is such a thing as constructive criticism.

If you ask high achievers about their own performance, they will be much more critical than you ever would dream of being. I remember observing a wonderful lesson—one of those magic moments in the classroom. In the post-observation conference, I opened the discussion by asking the teacher how she thought the class went. She spent several minutes picking apart a magnificent lesson! I finally interrupted her to focus on all the positive things I had observed. My praise enhanced our relationship; I was always welcome to observe in her classroom. She never stopped being judgmental of herself, but that is part of what made her special. I want to associate with teachers like her. They are the ones that make a good school great.

Autonomy and Recognition

When Al Burr (1993) discussed superstar teachers, he indicated that truly outstanding faculty members need two things to make them content and motivated: autonomy and recognition. Give your superstars autonomy—freedom to do the things they know are best. Let them take chances and risks. Watch them implement innovations that all the rest can draw from. As we mentioned earlier, don't require research before you cut one of your best teachers loose on a new idea. Instead, document the process and try to figure out how to get everyone else to implement it as well.

Giving our superstars autonomy also means that we do not attempt to control the behavior of less positive faculty members by establishing rules. Every time we put in a rule, the good people will follow it and thus lose autonomy. The others, for whom it was intended, will ignore it anyhow.

In addition to autonomy, give your high achievers recognition. This does not necessarily mean formal recognition. The Teacher of the Year award usually doesn't mean the teacher of the year anyhow. At best, it means the best teacher who hasn't won the award previously. Usually our best teacher is the same person every year. We just rotate the prize to be more inclusive.

Instead of an end-of-the-year award, consistently acknowledge that what your best teachers do is different and special. Let them know how much they mean to you and to the students. Write them notes, send them emails, drop Post-it[r] notes on their desks—in short, consistently reinforce their efforts. Though this may take some effort on your part, any energy you invest will earn compound interest. When we acknowledge the efforts of others, especially our highest achievers, they redouble their efforts. They feel more connected to us and to the school. When we show our respect for them, they gain more respect for us. Reinforcing our teachers—especially the ones we value most—makes everyone's job easier and more satisfying.

Teacher Evaluations

A major—and fascinating—aspect of my work with schools, principals, and districts involves teacher evaluation. What sparked my interest was the evaluation process in a district where I worked as a first-year principal. Some of the best teachers in the school—the teachers I most respected—told me confidentially that our evaluation process had limited value; some even considered it a joke.

Well, I don't know about you, but I am not secure enough to have my best teachers think there is little or no value to anything I do that involves them or takes up their time. With their guidance, I took a different approach to evaluation, even though I was still required to use the formal paperwork that the district mandated. However, one part of the process helped me understand high achievers and the importance of approaching them correctly.

One part of the process was a year-end summative checklist. A miniature version of the form looked something like this:

	Expectations		
	Below	Meets	Exceeds
1. The teacher manages student behavior appropriately.	_____	_____	_____
2. The teacher is well prepared for instruction.	_____	_____	_____
3. The teacher monitors student progress.	_____	_____	_____
4. The teacher follows the rules and policies of the district.	_____	_____	_____
5. The teacher . . .			

The form listed 20 criteria, with three choices for each: Below Expectations, Meets Expectations, and Exceeds Expectations. The third column—referred to as the "walk on water" column—was added years ago to reinforce the best teachers in a district, but ironically, it did just the opposite. If the highest of high achievers received Exceeds Expectations for 18 of 20 criteria (a world record, by the way), they were disappointed. They expect to exceed in *every* area; that's why they are high achievers.

The fact that no one else received even 12 WOWs makes no difference. Our best staff members do not often compare themselves with others. They compare themselves with perfection all the time. They expect to excel in everything they do. Telling them that they excel doesn't make them less motivated. Quite the opposite: They strive to do even more. High achievers thrive on positive recognition; anything less can be deflating.

What about Burnout?

A friend of mine used to say, "Teachers who say they are burned out were probably never on fire in the first place." There is more than a little truth to this, but we all know how many demands our high achievers face, from us and even more from themselves.

When there is a call for volunteers, their hands go up. If we need something done right, we ask them. We all face this temptation. However, it is essential that we protect our high achievers, not just from us, but from themselves.

Delegation is a difficult issue for principals. We have so much to do, and so little time. We struggle to balance the needs and our energies. When it comes to delegation, we are tempted to turn first to our best staff members. After all, they seem eager to volunteer, they get things done on time, and they get things done right, whether it be state visitation forms, parent newsletters, or district committees. They are always ready, willing, and most of all able. But is there no end to their time and energy?

A principal's rule of thumb for delegation is very simple: We must delegate anything that anyone else can do. If a secretary can do it, delegate; if our assistant can handle the task, pass it along. Why? Because there are so many things that *only the principal can do*.

We must use the same rule for our highest achievers and best staff members. Don't ask them to do anything that someone else can do—because there are so many things that *only our high achievers can do*. It's a mistake to ask an open-ended question at a faculty meeting: "Who would be willing to be on the social committee?" Predictably, everyone looks at their feet, you squirm for a minute or two, and eventually a superstar steps forward out of pity for you.

Unfortunately this has two results: Other staff members do not pull their weight, and the high achievers spend the time and energy they could put into innovative efforts that really make a difference to the school and the students. If we assign our best teachers many unimportant tasks, we waste a valuable resource. If we plan ahead and ask others to take on less essential tasks, we protect our high achievers and gain the involvement of other staff members.

This does not mean that you single out your best teachers by exempting them from the routine duties everyone shares. They don't want such favoritism. Rather, it means you tell them ahead of time when you *don't* want them to volunteer. High achievers put pressure on themselves; relieve them of it. Corner your superstars and ask them not to volunteer to coordinate the staff holiday party. Before they can feel insulted, tell them why: You are forming a curriculum committee that will shape the direction of the school, and you need them in that group. This approach reinforces your best teachers while allowing them not to feel guilty about staying away from a much less significant endeavor.

Great principals consistently pay attention to the needs of all their staff members, but they are particularly sensitive to the needs of their best teachers. Though these high achievers may sometimes demand more time and effort than other staff members in their quest for excellence, the rewards are immense. Conversely, high achievers are among the first to leave when they do not feel valued and important. We might think our gripers will be the first to go, but they seldom have other places that want them. Our best staff members can succeed anywhere, doing just about anything. If we do not take care of them, someone else will—and we will have squandered our most valuable resource.

14

Make It Cool to Care

Effective principals have a strong core of beliefs—principles that guide their decisions, touchstones that help them distinguish right from wrong, goals that define their vision for the school. I would like to share the core beliefs I followed in my years as a principal. I realize that these are personal; each of you must have your own core of beliefs. I outline my beliefs here for three reasons. One is just to let you know how simple they are. Another is to help build an understanding that the clearer our beliefs are, the more effective we can be in working toward them. A third is to illustrate how these core beliefs frame the way we work in schools.

Make It Cool to Care

My central goal was incredibly simple and incredibly complex. I wanted it to be "cool to care" in my school. I wanted everyone—every student, every teacher, each staff member, all the parents—to think it was cool to care. Ironically, I don't think I ever shared this goal with anyone—maybe because it sounded so simple, maybe because it might be scoffed at, and maybe to improve its chance of becoming reality. Chanting "Be drug free, you and me" during Red Ribbon Week may or may not make a difference, but I am pretty sure that when kids reach a certain age, its value diminishes. I felt the same about advertising my goal.

In this book, we have occasionally referred to trends in education. Some have had positive and lasting effects; others seem silly in hindsight. I regularly receive calls from schools and districts asking me to help them implement a program or reach a goal. Often, this undertaking relates to the latest trend or mandate. Whether I agree or not, I want the leaders to understand that getting a faculty to go along with a particular undertaking has limited value. Rather, the key is to develop and establish a school-wide environment that supports everyone's effort to do what is right. If we create an environment where each person does what is best for the students and for the school, we will seldom make a wrong decision. Getting people to do the current thing is fine. Getting people to do the right thing is essential.

The best teachers are able to achieve this in their classrooms. The students care, and they care deeply. They care about the curriculum, they care about learning, they care about the teacher, and they care about each other. Once it is cool to care, anything becomes possible. All the behaviors we have described in this book lead to this. Treating everyone with respect and dignity; always taking a positive approach; teaching the teachers how to treat the students; expecting loyalty to the students; understanding that what matters is people, not programs; hiring great teachers; making every decision based on the best people—each of these helps create an environment where it is cool to care. If two people both make every decision on what is best for students, even if they don't agree, they will both be right.

Once we create an environment where it is cool to care, there are no wrong decisions. People who make the extra effort are valued. Whining is worthless; caring is keen. Think about the very best teachers in your school. If they want to, they can make any new program work. No matter what the new standards are, they can help all their students meet them. The real challenge, and the real accomplishment, is to get all the students to care about what happens in the classroom. Once we achieve that, anything is possible. Until we achieve that, any obstacle can seem insurmountable.

The Great Teacher

In Chapter 1, I described my interest in understanding what great principals do differently. This interest extends to what great teachers do differently. The first time this struck me was during an informal visit in the classroom of my best teacher, Mrs. Heart. I watched as Darin approached her desk—Darin, a rough, tough, tattooed discipline problem who easily intimidated the other students (and many of the teachers, and maybe the principal!). Making no effort to keep the other students from hearing him, Darin said, "Mrs. Heart, I was working on my poetry last night and I had a hard time with some of the words in the third verse. I was wondering if I could get your help on . . ." My jaw must have hit the floor.

Believe me, Darin was not a fan of poetry. Darin was a fan of Mrs. Heart. She had made it cool to care about whatever was happening in class. No matter what the focus, the students shared that focus. When the state set new standards, I never worried about Mrs. Heart. She could get the students interested in whatever the state issue was, but she never lost sight of the big picture. Mrs. Heart wasn't preparing her students for the state test. Mrs. Heart was preparing her students for life. This is what teaching is all about. Getting along with others, treating everyone with respect, doing your best—that was Mrs. Heart. She made it cool to care.

As a principal, if I can raise every teacher to Mrs. Heart's level, or even close to that, I have something special. Even if my teachers are just trying to get there, that is wonderful. You see, if you want to be like Mrs. Heart, then you think it is cool to care.

Merry Christmas, Everyone!

One year the junior high school where I was principal decided to adopt a partner school—a preschool whose students had multiple handicaps, including severe disabilities. I was very proud of our students. They were pen pals to the youngsters, sent them cards on their birthdays, and hosted monthly theme parties.

As the holiday season approached, our students decided to do something special for their adoptees. They decided to raise money to buy each one a hat, mittens, and a sweatshirt with our school logo emblazoned across the front. The students came up with the idea of holding a half-hour carnival during our advisory time each morning for one week. Each day, one fifth of the homerooms would host the carnival and the other students would attend. Each group thought of different booths—ring toss games, root beer floats for a quarter, jars of candy to guess the number of pieces, even raffles to throw pies at the *assistant* principal (not me).

All the booths were inexpensive; our goal was to have each homeroom raise just $10. Well, the carnival was an unqualified success. Even the homerooms with resistant teachers who took a minimal role reached the $10 goal. We then pooled the money and bought the mittens, hats, and school sweatshirts.

Students in art classes made holiday cards for the preschoolers. Home Ec classes baked cookies. All the advisory teachers wrapped presents. Then came the day of the big party at the preschool. I had each homeroom teacher "randomly" select one student to help. (The faculty knew that in such situations, "random" meant the student who would benefit most.) The band played, the choir sang, the orchestra performed, and the drama students did holiday skits. I even chose a student to wear my personal Santa Claus suit and play St. Nick at the festivities. We caught the entire party on video—the severely disabled students sitting on Santa's lap (or as close as they could); everyone enjoying the music; our students comfortably and fearlessly holding and entertaining the preschoolers; excited children opening their presents. It was something special.

Two days later, as part of our traditional all-school holiday assembly, we wheeled out several large-screen televisions and played the tape of the party. Everyone got to see the love and joy that we brought into these youngsters' lives. They got to see the special children they had "adopted" look with amazement into Santa's eyes. Tears came easily when our students saw the video of these very challenged children hugging their classmates. By the time the tape ended, there were few dry eyes in the auditorium. And this was a group of junior high students!

Then, after the tape was over, the curtains opened on stage. There were all our very special preschool friends, in their matching sweatshirts with our school name and mascot, singing carols to us. No one in that room will ever forget it. You see, that is school.

We didn't have any fights in school the rest of the week; no one was even referred to the office. And we never had a problem with students teasing any of their own disabled peers who attended our junior high. The impact on the students was dramatic, but even more significant was the effect on our least positive staff members. After that, whenever we did something as a school, all the advisory teachers willingly rolled up their sleeves and joined in. Once it becomes cool to care, there are no limits to what can be accomplished.

Who Are the Legends?

In great schools, the teachers tell stories about what other teachers have accomplished with students. The heroes are not the contract-negotiating team, but those who have the greatest impact on the students. In one school I visited, the legendary figures were teachers who had students move in with them, and staff members who worked with children late into the night.

Some folks keep alive the legend of teachers who knock a student down with a single sarcastic comment; others revere those who pick the students up. Every principal needs to know which teachers are the legends. Effective principals work to make sure the ones on the pedestal are the best ones. Cultivating this environment is essential to developing a great school.

I recently worked with a school where unprofessional attitudes and behaviors were common. Faculty members put students down and thought that failing a student showed how good the teacher was. In trying to change this culture, I met with eight of the top teachers in the school and shared my concerns about the underlying attitude and tone. The nodded in agreement but were not sure what to do about it.

Eventually, one teacher asked if they should stand up to their negative peers. In response, I told them what one outstanding teacher did in a similar situation. At a dysfunctional school where I was the new principal, many on the staff habitually made sarcastic and derogatory remarks—not gentle teasing, but much more negative and usually hurtful. When this happened, one particular teacher's response stood out in my eyes. When her colleagues used inappropriate and hurtful humor, she didn't confront them—she simply didn't laugh.

"And that is what I need you to do too," I told the group of concerned teachers. "Just do what is right, no matter what others do around you." That is what the great teachers do, and the best principals. They do what is right no matter what else is going on.

Touch the Emotional Side

When working with schools that are attempting to implement change, I am continually amazed at how much time and energy principals put into presenting logical reasons why teachers should want to change their ways. There is nothing wrong with this, and I don't mean to be critical. But once we have presented the logical reasons clearly, those who resist change probably won't be swayed by further argument. Instead, we must realize that emotions play a part too. Often, the greatest impediment to change is fear—especially fear of the unknown. To overcome this obstacle, we have to rely on emotion ourselves.

Think about adults who are afraid of flying. We can present all sorts of facts about how flying is safer than driving, and it probably won't make any difference. They may even agree with us about the facts. They don't have a logical reason for staying on the ground; they are afraid. However, if an emergency arises and they need to be with a faraway family member quickly, they might readily decide to fly anyway. Their emotions overcome their irrational fear.

We can use the same approach when we are hoping to increase the sensitivity of our teachers to all their students. We can present logical reasons why each student deserves a teacher's attention and respect, but it's easy for resistant teachers to convince themselves that they can't work with one student, or several. How can we change their minds?

I know that in Chapter 9, I discussed at length the importance of focusing on behaviors before beliefs. I am not changing that view, but effective principals do not give up on altering beliefs. They understand that behaviors and beliefs are tied to emotion, and they understand the power of emotion to jump-start change.

I'll give you an example. When I became principal of an eighth-grade center (adolescence at its finest!), the tone in the school was less than positive. Several teachers did not hold students in the regard that I feel is essential. This attitude carried over to their classrooms and the way they treated and interacted with students, especially students who were less than teacher-pleasers in appearance or attitude.

The only thing I could think of was to attempt to reach the emotional side of the faculty. With the help of an outstanding high school counselor, we put together a panel of students who attended our school the previous year but who had not succeeded here—not major discipline or attendance problems, just pretty nice kids, the kind who easily fall through the cracks. They don't draw attention to themselves, but they are not interested in school, not involved, not connected.

Six students agreed to be panelists at a faculty meeting. The only prepping they received was to be honest. What happened over the next hour was unbelievably emotional. The students shared that they thought none of their teachers liked them. They thought no one cared. They were not even sure some of their teachers knew their names. It was quite sad. But, then, one of my coldest staff members blurted out, "Well, maybe if you had just done your homework you would have done better. Maybe if you had tried more you would have been more successful. Maybe if you had studied more you wouldn't have flunked my class!"

What happened next was powerful. Nothing happened. No one agreed. No one chimed in. I could almost sense the other teachers moving their chairs away from him. This teacher had moved from being a negative leader on the staff to total isolation. Maybe none of my other teachers stood up to him, but one thing they did sure made me proud. None of them laughed.

15

Don't Need to Repair—
Always Do Repair

In Chapter 4, we discussed treating everyone with respect and dignity every day. This is the standard that we must all work toward, and the very best principals come close. By the same token, most of us have worked with or for someone who was nice most of the time but would let the volcano erupt now and then. Unfortunately, some of these tantrums may have resulted in personal hurts that never totally healed.

When we, as leaders, lapse into such behaviors, we may never know the damage we have caused. If we become impatient and unprofessional, we are much more likely to throw darts. Though we may get over it, our targets may not. Sure, the people may still act hospitable toward us. After all, what choice do they have—especially if they fear being treated like that again? However, the relationship may never be the same. Effective principals understand this, so they aim to treat people with respect ten days out of ten. They know that a relationship, once damaged, may never be the same. That is one reason that effective people—both principals and teachers—are so acutely sensitive to every single thing they say and do. They work to avoid actions that cause hurt feelings. The most effective among us go beyond that.

Some Never Need to Repair—But Always Do

One of the things I notice about the best teachers is that they seldom engage in the behaviors that cause harm to students. They don't make cutting remarks or issue smart retorts. They don't run students down or embarrass them in front of their peers. Quite the opposite: The best teachers consistently compliment and praise students. Yet, though the best teachers seldom need to do any emotional repairing in their classrooms, they are continually working to repair, just in case.

Picture the most dynamic teachers in your school. They are the ones who are most likely to start off their class on a Tuesday morning by apologizing about something they did on Monday: "Class, I am sorry if I seemed a little impatient yesterday. I wasn't feeling well and I was running late. I wanted to let you know that I am sorry if I was a little short with any of you."

The class, of course, is sitting there with blank stares. They thought yesterday's class was great—actually, the best class they had all day. This shows not only the teacher's incredible sensitivity, but also the level of trust and credibility established with students. As we noted before, the best teachers have high expectations for others, but much higher expectations for themselves.

The best principals also work hard to keep their relationships in good repair, and teachers notice. In the previously mentioned study of more than 230 principals, Whitaker (1997) determined that the more effective principals were acutely aware of teacher strengths and supported individual staff development, needs, and desires. Additionally, the principals had a high knowledge of staff beyond school. They inquired about their families, personal lives, and outside interests.

This sensitivity leads effective principals to work to avoid personal hurt and to repair any possible damage. After a faculty meeting, the best principals might seek out a teacher to say something like, "I am sorry if I cut you off at the meeting. My mind jumped to another topic. Is there anything else you wanted to say?" Or after a conference, the principal, after having time to reflect, may revisit the teacher and add, "I hope I did not come across negatively. I wasn't sure that I handled my comments as sensitively as I could have."

In most cases, the teachers react with surprise. They thought the principal handled it well. They were not the least bit upset at the comments or their tone. However, they still appreciate the effort. And if the principal's behavior had bothered them, the effort to repair the relationship pays off.

Let's contrast this approach with that of the less effective teachers and principals.

Some Always Need to Repair—But Never Do

Think about the less skilled teachers in your school. Picture the ones who are most confrontational. Visualize their mannerisms, body language, and tone of voice. How do they treat the students when they are in a bad mood? Think of how they tread on students' feelings and self-worth. (Sorry to put you in a bad mood, but we needed to have specific individuals in mind.) Now, do they ever treat people, either students or adults, in a way that might hurt someone's feelings? Do they ever need to do some repair work? Of course. Unfortunately, you know this, and so does everyone else in their classrooms and in the school. The only ones who probably don't know this are the offenders themselves.

Intentionally or not, people like this regularly offend and insult others. Their reasons may not be as significant as their actions, especially to the person they just affronted. Yet these same individuals seldom recognize the need to repair. And more significantly, they seldom work to repair.

This has two implications for the principal. First, instead of focusing on getting them to admit they were wrong and/or to apologize, we really need to put our time and energies into helping build their "people skills" so that they do not do it again. Otherwise, we will constantly wrestle with the issue of repair. We must center our efforts on changing their approach so that they do not need to repair.

Second, however, we want to make it easier for them to repair. What keeps them from apologizing? Usually, what stands in the way is their lack of self-confidence or—often the flip side of the same coin—their pride or ego. We may not be able to deal with these issues directly, but if we can find a way that enables them to apologize, then we can change their behaviors without necessarily altering their beliefs. Let's take a look at one method.

I Am Sorry That Happened

In the book *Dealing with Difficult Parents (And with Parents in Difficult Situations)*, I describe a tool that a principal can use to defuse aggressive parents. No matter what the details of a situation, a principal can tell the parent, "I am sorry that happened." And the amazing thing is, it's really true. Any time I deal with a belligerent parent, regardless of the issue, I truly am sorry that it happened (whatever "it" is).

I am not saying it was my fault; I am not accepting or placing blame; I am just sorry that it happened. And the more offensive the parent is, the more sorry I am it happened! To myself I am adding, "I sure am sorry it happened, otherwise I wouldn't be spending this time with you!" Of course we would never share our private thoughts with these people, and we must always maintain a professional attitude. Nevertheless, the simple statement "I am sorry that happened" is a powerful defusing technique.

Of course, this is not limited to parents. Any time anyone shares bad news with me, I really am sorry it happened. If a teacher's grant application is turned down, "I am so sorry that happened." If a child falls and skins her knee, "I am so sorry that happened." Again, I am not saying that I tripped her, I am just sorry it happened.

Every principal reading this book may already know and use this approach. But the real challenge is not developing and practicing this skill ourselves, but *teaching our teachers* the skill. If they learn to use it regularly, we will have to do a lot less repairing on their behalf. In particular, if our most negative teachers can master this skill, what a service to them—and to us and to our school.

So, we might start by suggesting that if a parent is attacking them, regardless of the circumstances they should be able to say, professionally and with empathy, "I am so sorry that happened." With our most resistant staff, we might share a little more of our internal dialogue. If they need to add *to themselves*, "because otherwise I wouldn't be spending my time with you," that's okay. After all, we don't need to like the parent; we only need to act that way. They can even add *to themselves*, "As a matter of fact, I am a little sorry you moved into our district!" This is probably something we have all felt at times.

Of course, we must emphasize that as professionals, we can *never* be sarcastic or demeaning in our tone of voice or body language. However, on the inside we can be whatever we want. After all, what we most need these teachers to do is to change their behavior. And if they change for selfish reasons, that doesn't matter. The critical issue isn't *why* but *whether* they changed their behavior.

Not only do we need to develop and refine these skills in every staff member, but we can also reap great benefits if we teach them to our students.

The Highway Patrol

We have identified skills that we know are important to being a successful professional. As educators, we need to work to develop these abilities in our students. Some of our students have them to some degree, but many have not been exposed to them at all. For them, teachers who regularly practice the skill of repairing can serve as an important role model. But in addition to modeling the skill, we may also need to teach it.

As principals, we have many opportunities to teach this skill. Think of all the students who are referred to the office for being uncooperative or argumentative with a teacher. Now, with all discipline matters, it is essential that we focus on prevention, not punishment. We can't do anything about the fact that the incident occurred; the only thing we can do is try to prevent it from happening again. However, we do know that each student can work to repair the current situation. This is our opportunity to help them learn how repairing relations can be to *their* advantage.

Let's pretend Johnny gets sent to the office out of Mrs. Smith's class. When he arrives, you ask him, "Johnny, what happened?" He responds that Mrs. Smith sent him to the office for arguing with her. The referral form he brought confirms his story. You ask him to walk you through what happened. Then you ask him, "Was Mrs. Smith mad?" Johnny affirms the obvious, "Yeah, she was real mad." So you get ready to share with Johnny the story of the highway patrol.

"Johnny, I am not going to decide your consequence until I go and talk to Mrs. Smith in person." (This sound practice should be a habit. It is part of making teachers *feel* supported.) "And Johnny, I won't have a chance to see her until after lunch. So, if I were in your shoes, when the bell rings at the end of this class period I would hightail it down to Mrs. Smith's classroom and I'd apologize. I would say something like [you are about to give Johnny the *specific* language to use], 'Mrs. Smith, I am sorry that . . . .'"

Why must you give Johnny the word-for-word language? Because he may not have it himself. Telling someone to do something without teaching him how makes no sense at all. So you teach him what to say. Now, how do you actually get him to do it? Simple: You make it a benefit to *him* to do it.

You continue with the dialogue. "And Johnny, I'm not asking you to go and apologize for my sake. And you don't even have to apologize for Mrs. Smith's sake. It's up to you—but if I were you, I would apologize for your *own* sake." "For me?" Johnny asks. "Yes, for you." This is where the highway patrol comes in.

"If I am driving down the highway and I get pulled over by a patrolman, when that patrolman is walking toward my car I have one goal. What is that goal?"

"To get out of the ticket."

"That's right. And I have two choices in my behavior: I can be nice, or I can be rude. Which is more likely to get me out of the ticket?"

"Being nice."

"And you know that my goal in being nice is selfish. It isn't to help the state revenue department. It isn't to help the highway patrolman. It is to help *me*—by making it more likely I will get out of the ticket. So if I were you, when that bell rings I'd scoot on down to Mrs. Smith's class and I would say something like . . . " [you give him the language again, just to ensure that he has it].

"And you said Mrs. Smith was mad, didn't you?"

"Yep, real mad."

"Well, if you want to see her mad again, just tell her that you're apologizing because I told you to. Now you do what you want, but if I were in your shoes I'd head down to Mrs. Smith's class when that bell rings and I would apologize."

The bell rings, and guess what Johnny does? He heads down to Mrs. Smith and apologizes. When you see her after lunch, you ask what happened with Johnny. She says that he came down and apologized and everything is fine. Whose job just got easier? Yours, of course!

Now you may still need to give Johnny a consequence, because 25 other students saw his behavior. Yet you can still reinforce him by saying, "Because you apologized I am only going to . . . ." This way you still encourage the apology. And what if Johnny doesn't go and see Mrs. Smith? You have lost nothing. It didn't work this time, but you never know when it might work in the future.

Some students already have the skill of repairing. If three kids in a class are talking inappropriately, the teacher might say something like, "Guys, let's quiet down." The reactions of the three students are likely to determine whether this situation is resolved or not. One of the students says, "Sorry," and gets quiet (good repairing skills). One student just goes silent and looks down. The third retorts, "We weren't the only ones talking!" and it goes back and forth from there. Now, our most effective teachers would ignore the remark and it would go away. However, we may have some staff members who don't yet have that skill, or maybe the student caught the teacher in the wrong mood, so matters escalate until the office is involved. Now, the principal has a teachable moment.

If we take this opportunity to teach students the *behaviors* that repair a situation instead of escalating it, our job becomes easier—and their lives become better. After all, no matter what professions our students enter, they will probably need to deal with supervisors; the way they respond could determine whether they succeed in that job (to say nothing of their encounters with the highway patrol).

I also realize that if we build the skills in each one of our teachers, they will not be part of this escalation process. But, in the meantime, developing these repairing skills in our students can help alleviate problems in all our classes. More importantly, we have taught them one of the skills of the most effective people in all professions.

16

Set Expectations at the Start of the Year

A school year is a journey that takes many different turns. One of the most exciting aspects of being a principal is that each day is so different. One of the most challenging aspects of being a principal is that each day is so different. I love the cycle of the school year, beginning with the anticipation, excitement, and energy of the first day. Standardized testing, pre-holiday events, the time before and after seasonal vacations, the dark days of winter, the first days of spring—each part has its own feel, its own dynamic ebb and flow, its own highlights and challenges. A school year has a personality all its own. There is a start, a middle, and an end. Few occupations are so cyclical.

The excitement of starting a new school year provides opportunities to reestablish expectations and introduce changes. We're all on our best behavior, full of positive energy about the coming year. For effective principals, the start of the year is a chance to set the tone for the school year and, more importantly, for the school. Even if we have been in the same building for several years, the opening of school is a new opportunity to move our faculty forward.

We Are Still Undefeated

Every school should have its Back-to-School Night before the year starts, or at the latest, on the evening of the first or second day of school. The reason is very simple—we are still undefeated. Students have not been "in trouble" (whatever that means). None of us are behind in our work. Nobody has any grades in the grade book. We have the chance to build new relationships. Like every major league baseball team in spring training, we can dream of making it to the World Series.

The start of the year is "prime time" for setting expectations about classroom management. Here we find the sharpest contrast between the most effective and the least effective teachers. Great teachers are very clear about their approach to student behavior. It can be summed up in one word: prevention. Great teachers do not want inappropriate behavior to occur. They establish clear expectations at the start of the year and follow them consistently as the year progresses. The consequences are either irrelevant or clearly secondary to the expectations. For example, a teacher might have three guidelines:

1. Be respectful.
2. Be prepared.
3. Be on time.

or

1. Respect yourself.
2. Respect others.
3. Respect your school.

The teacher may have predetermined and stated consequences, but that's not the point. The key is to set expectations and then establish relationships so that students want to meet these expectations.

In contrast, the approach of our least effective teachers to classroom management or discipline can often be summed up in one word: revenge. Ineffective teachers are motivated *after* a student misbehaves, to punish the student. If a child does not bring a pencil to class, they want that child to feel badly about it and choose to behave better as a result. Ineffective teachers consistently focus on the consequences as the fence that keeps students under control and doing what they should.

If a student misbehaves, great teachers want it not to happen again. They focus on the future. Poor teachers want to know what is going to happen to the student who misbehaved. They focus on the past.

As principals, we have a responsibility to support our teachers. This is essential. However, while we support a teacher in a discipline matter, we can also teach a different approach to discipline. Keep in mind, of course, that teachers do not just want to *be* supported; they want to *feel* supported, which may not be the same. Also realize that unless we shift a teacher's mindset away from revenge, that teacher will never feel supported, because any revenge is never enough.

Let's consider how teachers might want a student to behave after a disciplinary conference with the principal. Ineffective teachers want students to be upset when they leave the office. Effective teachers want students to be better when they leave. As a principal, I worked hard to help my teachers understand that we do not want students angry when they leave. Heck, they were angry when they got there. As a matter of fact, that may be why they were referred to the office in the first place. Angry students are a problem, not a solution.

As a school, we must seek a different solution: students who don't repeat their misbehavior. This may—and often does—require consequences. Plus, the consequences one student faces may prevent other students who witnessed the misbehavior from doing something similar. However, the point of consequences is not to make a student feel bad. The critical element is not how a student feels, but how a student behaves. This same approach applies to our teachers.

Why Every Year?

School leaders sometimes mistakenly assume that new staff members will absorb the culture and climate of the school through osmosis. True, new staff members will make some assumptions about "how things are supposed to be done around here," but unless the principal and others provide appropriate guidance, the assumptions may not be correct. Plus, even some returning or veteran staff members may not instinctively do things the most effective or most appropriate way.

Think of your teenagers leaving the house on a Friday night. Of course they know your expectations; they've had 17 years to learn them. Yet somehow it doesn't hurt to give them the positive reminders: "Be home by midnight," or "Remember your last name," or "Don't hesitate to call if you need anything." They have heard the same refrains many times; but we do hope that when they face challenging decisions, these words will help them make good choices.

I am sure that every teacher could rattle off a list of good classroom practices. And most of us follow them, most of the time. Yet, when we get tired or worn down, sometimes we revert to old habits that may not be the best. When certain students push our buttons, it might be hard to resist yelling at them or firing off a sarcastic comment. As principals, we ought to express clear expectations at the first faculty meeting of the year, when we are still undefeated. This sets an important benchmark that we can revisit if people go astray later in the school year. Effective principals also incorporate these expectations in the *Friday Focus* (Whitaker et al.) weekly staff memo, at monthly staff meetings, and in other interactions to keep them fresh in everyone's mind. Let's look at an example involving classroom management expectations for all teachers in a school.

Teacher Expectations for Classroom Management

Every principal will emphasize different goals and expectations. Effective principals establish expectations that express their core beliefs—their nonnegotiables. One of mine—in fact, perhaps the heart of my core beliefs—is the importance of how we treat students and interact with them every day. I thought I would share with you an exercise I used as a principal and still use with other groups of teachers.

As a principal, each year at the first faculty meeting I talked with teachers about managing student behavior. I began with this statement: "I cannot control the students' behavior in your classrooms." I always said this for one reason: It was true. I would then add, "But I will do everything I can to help you manage the students' behavior in your classroom." Then I would lead the staff through this exercise.

I start by asking, "What can teachers do when a student misbehaves in a classroom?" Not just what they would do, or what a good teacher would do, but all the options. As we brainstorm, I list their responses on a transparency or flip chart. I've done this with many groups, and the lists look remarkably similar: eye contact, proximity, redirect the student, send them to the office, put them in timeout, argue with the student, send them to sit in the hall, yell, ignore, praise another student for positive behavior, embarrass them, and so on.

(Now, most of you probably flinch at some of these behaviors and nod in agreement with others. However, the point here is quantity. After we generate a list, we can shift to quality.)

Then I ask the teachers, "Which of these approaches *always* work?" After some initial thought, the group invariably settles on the only correct answer, "None of them." Of course there is no one approach that always works. If there were, we would use it every time.

I describe these options as a teacher's bag of tricks. I ask, "Does every teacher have the same options?" The group usually understands that every teacher has the same tools in their bag of tricks. Every teacher can use eye contact or proximity, send a student to the office, praise, argue, or yell. Not every teacher does, but any teacher *could* do everything on this list and any other ideas that your staff can generate.

What, then, is the difference between good classroom managers and poor classroom managers? It's not what is in our bag of tricks; they are all the same. The variable is how often the teachers reach into their bag of tricks. A great teacher reaches in once or twice a day. A poor teacher grabs away several times an hour, and if we reach into our bag of tricks often enough, we're going to pull out some ugly ones.

Year after year, I found that this exercise helped me and my teachers to focus (or refocus) on prevention rather than reaction. No single reaction will work every time. We have to center our efforts on preventing misbehavior, just as the best teachers do.

I then take this one step further. I mention three of the things that are on the list: yelling, arguing, and humiliating (sarcasm). If one of these does not make the teacher-generated list, I still mention it as something important to me. Then I ask the teachers several questions. The reasons I ask rather than tell are very simple. One is that I know from experience what they will say. The second reason is that the responses generate expectations, and they are the teachers' expectations for themselves and each other—which are much more powerful than the principal's expectations for them.

You might use this same exercise to establish expectations at the start of the year. Ask your teachers the following questions:

"When is sarcasm appropriate in the classroom?" They know the answer: "Never." Once they express this, you respond, "Then let's never use it in our classrooms." This is an expectation, and best of all it is the teachers' expectation, not just yours.

Ask: "Who decides how many arguments you get into in a week?" The answer, of course, is, "We do." Then share this thought: We never win an argument with a student. As soon as it starts, we have lost. If their peers are watching, they cannot afford to give in. We would *like* to win the argument, but they *have* to win the argument. (Plus, I have always felt that in all student–teacher interactions, there needs to be at least one adult—and I would prefer that it be the teacher.) As a school, we also understand that we do not get into arguments with parents, central office, or anyone else. This has nothing to do with giving in or giving up. Not at all. It's a matter of being professional.

Finally, address yelling: "Outside of a true emergency— *Watch out for the acid!*—there is no place for yelling. The students we are most tempted to yell at have been yelled at so much, why on earth would we think this would be effective with them?"

Thus, we do not yell at students. (Here's another place for the comment about every situation needing at least one adult.)

Do you see why it is so important to do this at the start of the year? So far, nobody has yelled at Jimmy, argued with Mrs. Monster-Mom, or fired off a sarcastic comment. We are all still undefeated. If we wait until the second week of school, there is some chance that we will be describing previous behaviors, not establishing new and appropriate future expectations. Additionally, some teachers will revert to their "But you don't know what Jimmy is like in my class" mode. Then we are in a more reactionary struggle.

If we have established these guidelines in advance, we can refer to them when we need to. If we make it clear ahead of time that yelling, arguing, and sarcasm are inappropriate to use with students, then at the very least, teachers who lapse into this behavior know they are wrong. If we wait until after the fact, the teacher is on the defensive—and our least effective staff members often are the most defensive and guarded.

Now, your beliefs and expectations may differ from mine, and that's great. Maybe you would like less griping in the teachers' workroom (Whitaker 1999); it might be nice to have more hallway supervision; perhaps you would like to encourage more staff attendance at extracurricular events. You have to decide your personal needs and desires. The point of the exercise I just shared is that setting expectations at the start of the year is both reasonable and fair. What's not fair is to expect people to adhere to your expectations if you don't establish them up front. What's more, if you haven't clearly identified your expectations at the start of the year, they may be perceived as your expectations, not the school's expectations.

Great teachers establish expectations at the very beginning of the year; so do great principals. What is the variable? Not the specifics of the expectations, but that they are clearly established, focus on the future, and are consistently reinforced. All principals can do this. The great ones do.

17

Clarifying Your Core

Every principal's experience is unique, and every school is different. But great principals—regardless of student clientele, grade levels, or school size—have much in common. This book has highlighted fifteen hallmarks of great principals—their attitudes, goals, decisions, and practices. In the end, the difference lies in the core of beliefs that guide great principals' work. In this book, I have blended findings from several studies with conclusions drawn from less formal observations and interactions. More than that, I have shared the core of what matters to me.

I hold fast to certain essential beliefs. I'm convinced that the principal is the filter for whatever happens in a school. I believe that to improve your school, you must improve the teachers you have, or hire better teachers. I recognize that in any school, some programs work more successfully than others—but I'm sure that success comes from people, not programs. I insist on the importance of treating every person with respect and dignity, every single day.

On the other hand, some aspects of the day-to-day routine of school don't matter much to me. I have always worked to be punctual, but I never kept close tabs on whether my teachers arrived by the official check-in time, as long as they were effective with their students.

In my first years as a teacher, the principal required us all to turn in our lesson plans each week. I diligently did so, spending extra time to write them neatly and work for continuity. I also remember that as a result, I spent less time actually planning and preparing for class.

When I became a principal, I too collected lesson plans from my teachers—for about two weeks. But on reflection, I realized that what mattered was not neat lesson plans for me, but effective lesson plans for the students. At least at first glance, there was little connection between an effective teacher and a tidy plan book. When I thought about my best teachers, I realized they must see this requirement as just another hassle. What's more, I had asked for lesson plans only because someone else did—and I hadn't chosen a good role model. Of course, I have nothing against planning for lessons, and it might be a good idea to review the lesson plans of a poorly prepared teacher. But I decided not to take time and energy away from what mattered—engaging with students effectively.

Being a principal is an amazing profession. It is challenging, dynamic, energizing, and draining—but most of all, it is rewarding. Our impact extends far beyond anything we can imagine. We know that our teachers talk about us; so do people throughout our community. We can decide what we want those conversations to be like.

Every principal feels the pressure of outside influences. Everyone in the community has a vested interest in schooling—and everyone who ever went to school can claim to be an expert. This is not a criticism, just a fact of human nature. However, as principals we must adhere to our core values. No matter what others want us to do, we must focus on what is right for our students.

Like other leaders, principals can be lonely. Though we work in a community of colleagues, at times we have to make decisions on our own. Without a core of firmly held beliefs, it's difficult to steer a steady course. With this core, we feel secure and confident. And so do our teachers. And most importantly, so will our students.

This book does not present a cookie-cutter approach to leadership or a narrow doorway to success. Instead, it shows the framework that sustains the work of all great principals.

Think of it as a blueprint. The principals are the architects. The teachers establish the foundation. The students move into the building and fill it with life and meaning.

Every principal has an impact. Great principals make a difference.

References

Bissell, B. (1992, July). *The paradoxical leader.* Paper presented at the Missouri Leadership Academy, Columbia, MO.

Burr, A. (1993, September). *Being an effective principal.* Paper presented at the regional satellite meeting of the Missouri Leadership Academy, Columbia, MO.

Fiore, D. (1999). *The relationship between principal effectiveness and school culture in elementary schools.* Doctoral dissertation, Indiana State University, Terre Haute, IN.

Roeschlein, T. (2002). *What effective middle school principals do to impact school climate.* Doctoral dissertation, Indiana State University, Terre Haute, IN.

Turner, E. (2002). *What effective principals do to improve instruction and increase student achievement.* Doctoral dissertation, Indiana State University, Terre Haute, IN.

Whitaker, M. E. (1997). *Principal leadership behaviors in school operations and change implementations in elementary schools in relation to climate.* Doctoral dissertation, Indiana State University, Terre Haute, IN.

Whitaker, T. (1993). *Middle school programs and climate: The principal's impact.* Doctoral dissertation, University of Missouri–Columbia.

Whitaker, T. (1999). *Dealing with difficult teachers.* Larchmont, NY: Eye On Education.

Whitaker, T., & Fiore, D. (2001). *Dealing with difficult parents (and with parents in difficult situations).* Larchmont, NY: Eye On Education.

Whitaker, T., Whitaker, B., & Lumpa, D. (2000). *Motivating and inspiring teachers: The educational leader's guide for building staff morale.* Larchmont, NY: Eye On Education.

If you would like information about inviting
Todd Whitaker to speak to your group,
please contact him at **t-whitaker@indstate.edu**
or his Web site **www.toddwhitaker.com**
or (812) 237-2904.